FIRESIDE

Kurt Thomas
ON GYMNASTICS

By Kurt Thomas and Kent Hannon

Photographs by Rafael Beer

A Fireside Book
Published by Simon and Schuster
New York

Designed by Martin S. Moskof with Susan Gravdahl

Manufactured in the United States of America
Printed and Bound by The Murray Printing Company
1 2 3 4 5 6 7 8 9 10

Library of Congress Cataloging in Publication Data

Thomas, Kurt.
Kurt Thomas on gymnastics.

1. Gymnastics. 2. Thomas, Kurt. 3. Gymnasts—
United States—Biography. I. Hannon, Kent, joint
author. II. Title.
GV461.T44   796.4'1   80–10
ISBN 0–671–24798–0
ISBN 0–671–25508–8 Pbk.

For Beth and Sharron

Introduction

God, I should say,
has given men two arts,
music and gymnastics.

— Plato

Until recently, when my co-author Kurt Thomas began to bring the crowds to life, most men's gymnastics meets in this country were conducted in relative silence. Not the respectful kind of silence accorded the server in tennis, or the nervous, fingernail-biting variety that hangs in the air as Nicklaus stands over a putt at Augusta. This was an interested but slightly dumbfounded silence such as you might expect from an audience watching a foreign film without subtitles.

This book endeavors to put an end to that silence once and for all, and to replace it with the usual range of cheers, boos and opinionated emotion that the average American sports fan emits when he is watching something he not only enjoys but understands.

For the picture of men's gymnastics which emerges from these pages, we would like to thank all those people—gymnasts, coaches, administrators and journalists—who spoke so candidly about the nature of a sport in transition from cult status to mainstream popularity. We would especially like to acknowledge the help and cooperation we received from Roger Counsil, Ed McKee and Indiana State University; Rich Kenney, Tom Sauters and International Gymnast magazine; Frank Bare, Mas Watanabe and the United States Gymnastics Federation; Don Gutzler, Karl Schwenzfeier, Abe Grossfeld, Ken Allen, Gordon Maddux, Rusty Mitchell, Bill Meade, Frank Cumiskey and, of course, Gene Wettstone.

Kent Hannon
Kurt Thomas

Part One

Training

The little gym at Indiana State University may be the largest sauna in America. There isn't a window in the place, much less a breath of fresh air, and on an Indian summer afternoon when the temperature in Terre Haute is in the seventies, it gets insufferably hot within these bare, concrete walls. Just walking in and out reduces you to the perspiration level of those who torture themselves inside. So most people, even the most curious onlookers, don't come any closer than the doorway. It's not only cooler, it's safer.

The six-foot-three, 245-pound behemoth standing there right now, the one blocking the path of any little breeze which might bring a moment's relief from the heat, is an offensive tackle on the Indiana State football team. He is pictured in the Sycamore program and he looks mean. *In the program* he looks mean. In the doorway of the little gym he looks intimidated, maybe even a bit frightened—as though he can identify with the plight of the guy whose body is shaking with exertion up on the rings, or with the guy who just did several impressive somersaults in a row before going splat on the blue AMF mat. A stranger's question rescues the football player from these vicarious thrills.

"Ever try gymnastics?"

"My job is to protect the quarterback," says the tackle. "Until now I thought it was a pretty foolish occupation. But I'll take it any day over gymnastics. This shit is *bad!*"

In the vernacular of today's athletes, when something is described as *bad*, it is one of two things: so irresistible that you want to go crazy over it or so dangerous that you want to back off it altogether for fear it will hurt you. Either way, the description fits men's gymnastics.

The basic appeal of the sport is that it's 100 percent offense. A man with no 245-pound tackles to protect him goes out and attacks six different apparatus—the rings, high bar, pommel horse, parallel bars, long horse vault, and floor exercise mat—in hopes of scoring close enough to 10.0 on each that eventually he can work his way up to the Olympic All-Around title. That's the

Mount Everest challenge in men's gymnastics. By the same token, these six apparatus are notorious for putting the gymnast on the defensive.

The young gymnast struggling through a rings routine over in the corner is no All-Arounder. He is just a pommel horse specialist, which means he spends fifteen to twenty hours a week working solely on the horse. It is the only event in which he ever competes. He would like to be an All-Arounder, but at the moment he is just a hacker on the other five events. Clearly, he has no business on the rings. He is trying to do what is called an iron cross. It's a move everybody recognizes: You look like you're being crucified. But if he doesn't give up on it pretty soon, his sagging body weight may tear his bicipital tendon away from his shoulder.

"Hey, why don't you get off there before you hurt yourself!"

The booming words of advice come not from Roger Counsil, the Indiana State coach, but from a fresh-faced kid standing next to the trampoline who looks the American ideal of Little Brotherdom. His fluffy, center-parted hair and easy smile are reminiscent of Shaun Cassidy, but there is something about the intensity of those brown eyes in combination with that broad back and shoulders that suggests a streak of daredeviltry. Whoever the kid is, he is something of a contortionist because his left foot is resting on the frame of the trampoline at a seemingly impossible angle next to his left ear. Nor is he through giving orders. Another gymnast staggering through a routine over on the high bar has caught his eye.

"Release it harder, you skid!"

The kid doing all the coaching from the sidelines is Kurt Thomas, and despite the teenager's face he is no kid. He is twenty-two years old and has a wife to prove it. If he seems to treat the little gym at Indiana State like his private domain, it is because he is by far the finest gymnast, male or female, that the United States has ever produced. And while that distinction has not

meant much in the past, what with the United States's heretofore dismal showings in international gymnastics competition, it is about to.

This is the start of a red-letter month for Thomas. Tonight—Thursday, October 5, 1978—he will appear on the Merv Griffin show in Hollywood. But through the magic of videotape, he will be sitting home in his trailer on the outskirts of Terre Haute as several million Americans are marveling at his demonstration of the Thomas Flair.

The Flair is a whirling, helicopter-like move on pommel horse that bears Thomas's name because he was the first man to unveil it in an international meet. Gymnasts all over the world are going crazy over it, even though no one—not even the Indiana State pommel horse specialist—can do it quite like Kurt. This marks only the second time in a century of gymnastics history that a trick has been named for an American. In the last twenty years, nearly every addition to the repertoire has been supplied by either a Japanese or a Russian—a *Tsukahara* vault, an *Endo*-shoot on high bar, a *Diamidov* on parallel bars, a *Veronin* on high bar—because they have been the greatest innovators in the sport. To find judges awarding points for how well a man performs the *Thomas* Flair is quite an anomaly.

On Tuesday, Thomas will leave for Europe and the World Gymnastics Championships in Strasbourg, France, where he will try to prove to the Russians and Japanese that an American is on the way to becoming the best gymnast in the world. For him to succeed would be no more unusual than finding the next O. J. Simpson in Chile.

Thomas's teammates don't mind his calling them "skids" when they screw up. It's a remnant of his own Miami, Florida, street vernacular and ordinarily he uses it as a perverse term of affection. Besides, none of them has posed for pictures with royalty as Kurt did when he and Nadia Comaneci took their victory bows at the 1977 Romanian Invitational. None of them has won a

National Collegiate Athletic Association title or three straight United States Gymnastics Federation championships as Kurt has. And certainly none of them can claim to have put men's gymnastics on the map—and near the top in the Nielsen ratings—the way Kurt did when he won all six events with scores of 9.6 or higher at the 1978 Dial-American Cup in Madison Square Garden.

That Sunday, March 12, was a pivotal day for men's gymnastics because ABC was televising the American Cup as part of its *Wide World of Sports* show. The rating for the American Cup segment was 14.5, equivalent to 30,000,000 viewers or roughly twice the audience of any golf or tennis show ABC had telecast in the preceding year. Thomas's performance and the ratings it produced convinced network executives that they had just witnessed the debut of a new international sports star, a male gymnast with the right kind of looks and charisma to capture American hearts just as Olga Korbut had done six years earlier at the Munich Olympics. All three TV networks have been covering his every move ever since. Thus, in one afternoon Thomas did something for men's gymnastics that took Billie Jean, Pelé, Broadway Joe, and Dr. J years to do for their outcast sports or leagues.

All of the underclassmen in the little gym say they came to Indiana State to have a chance to train with Kurt. So if he decides to get on somebody's case, the guy usually considers it an honor. And in a sport as technically demanding as gymnastics, having the opportunity to watch an athlete of Thomas's caliber work an apparatus for even five minutes is worth a week of coaching tips—and Counsil would be the first to agree.

For an All-Arounder, every workout is like an army physical. Each of the six events that comprise a gymnastics program is a different station; you spend at least half an hour at each one and by the end of the day you're chafed, callused, and bedraggled. The rings is probably the most strenuous of the six events, so Thomas will start there.

A long time exposure in a light-controlled setting produced this photograph of the Thomas Flair, a pommel horse maneuver in which Kurt paws the air with his feet while supporting himself on one arm and then the other. Thomas introduced the Flair in Barcelona in 1975 and is only the second American in a century to have a gymnastics move named after him.

Gymnasts are out on the mat a full hour before practice begins in order to get their bodies stretched out and loosened up.

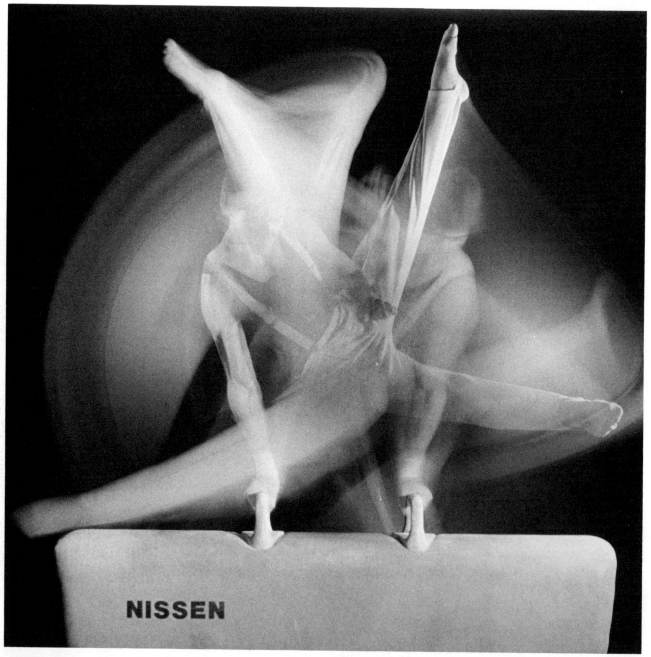

NISSEN

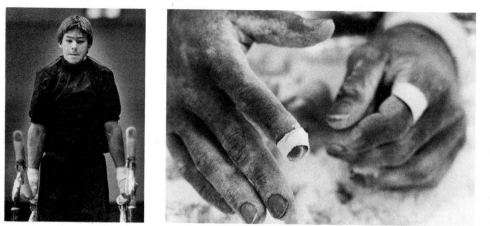

It is 4 P.M. and up until now the little gym has been quiet and passive. Since 3:05, Thomas and his teammates have been flopped down on the mats doing their stretching exercises. This is a time for kneading the other guy's feet and shoulders, for doing the splits, and for turning oneself into a human pretzel in order to get limbered up for what is to follow. It is also an occasion for swapping international trivia via the foreign language that only gymnastics people understand.

"I hear Kajiyama mounts with a full-twisting double back on floor."

"Yeah, and then what?"

"Roundoff, flip-flop, whip back. He finishes with a double back."

"What about his third pass?"

"Don't know. But I hear he dismounts with a triple twister."

It is hard for anyone to get motivated in this heat, and the scene is made even more languid by the fact that Indiana State's college season doesn't begin for another five weeks. Counsil hasn't come in yet, either, thanks to a long-winded call from some Hollywood agent who wants to make Kurt a star.

"By now I've lost track of who all these people are and whom they represent," says Counsil, finally making his appearance in the gym. "I don't know if this was the Bee Gees' guy or Bill Bixby's or Bruce Jenner's. But it seems to me that Kurt is already a star."

He certainly is the whole show at Indiana State, because it isn't until he gets a boost up to the rings, which hang 8½ feet off the ground, that those bare, concrete walls begin to rock with sound. For one thing, someone has resurrected the team's stereo receiver from the storage closet, dusted off the layer of magnesium carbonate that covers the FM dial, and found a station playing Earth, Wind & Fire. Magnesium carbonate—or chalk, as it is usually called—is the white, powdery substance that gymnasts use on their hands to reduce friction and make sure they get a good grip on the apparatus. It covers everything in the Indiana State gym like a blanket of snow. Gymnasts don't do anything, with the possible exception of going to the bathroom, without first "chalking up." Usually this is a simple matter of survival, but the chalk box is also a good place to commiserate with a teammate about the condition of your hands—to see which calluses are about to pop and which ones are already bleeding.

Another reason the gym has suddenly come alive is that Thomas is the only Indiana State gymnast who qualified for the World Championships in France. It is the most important meet in gymnastics, other than the Olympics, and his teammates want to give him a big sendoff.

"Awwwright, Kurt, let's go!"

"Take it to the max!"

"Get psyched!"

Thomas manipulates the ten feet of steel and canvas cable which connects the rings to the top of the apparatus as easily as if it were a jump rope. He warms up with a "giant swing." From one motionless handstand, he loops down and back up to another with no visible signs of exertion. However, with the biggest meet of his life so close at hand, he is taking no chances on wiping out. Around his waist he wears a heavy leather safety belt to which two long, white ropes are attached. The ropes extend up to a pair of pulleys at the top of the rings frame and then back down to the floor, where Counsil and one of Thomas's teammates have hold of the ends. The system works on the same principle as the dual sets of controls in a driver-education car. If a gymnast wants to work on a new trick he is unsure of, or needs to inject some new life into an old one without fear of the consequences, he can put on the safety belt and throw caution to the wind. If he gets in trouble on his dismount and looks like he's about to crash, the people down below just give a yank on the ropes and—*voila!*—he can be braked to a halt a couple of feet above the mat.

Thomas looks like a man who spends fifteen to

twenty hours a week on the rings alone, not twenty to thirty minutes per day, and nobody has to yank him to safety as he lands his first half-in, half-out dismount. It is a wicked-looking move in that between the time he lets go of the rings and his feet hit the mat, he must execute a front somersault *and* a back somersault. It sounds like a superhuman feat far beyond the powers of mortal men, but Thomas tries to explain the secret while he chalks up and prepares to do another.

"It looks like I'm turning myself inside out, I know," he says. "But while I'm flipping end-over-end in the front somersault, I'm also twisting my body lengthwise a half turn. That way, when I complete the first somersault I'm facing the opposite way as when I started, and I just automatically flow into a back somersault. I don't know . . . maybe it's easier to do than to describe!"

To an untrained eye, Thomas's second half-in, half-out looks like a carbon copy of the first. But somewhere in the middle of it, he decides to bail out and do it over. He gives a yelp for help, Counsil tugs on the rope, and he is left floating harmlessly in space à la Mary Martin in *Peter Pan.*

Kurt looks like a boy who never grew up. At five feet five and 126 pounds he is small enough that his wife, Beth, can wear his clothes. But if ever anyone found his niche in life, it is Thomas. In gymnastics, small is beautiful. The Japanese have proved that axiom by fielding the shortest, lightest, and best men's gymnastics teams in the world since 1960. Their gold-medal-winning team at the 1976 Olympics averaged five feet three and 130 pounds, the most diminutive lineup of any country. So while Thomas may look like a shrimp to the outside world, in the little gym at Indiana State he is average sized. The biggest guy in the place is five-foot-nine, 140 pounds—unless you count Counsil, a congenial walrus who was once Athlete of the Year at Southern Illinois University, but whose days as a champion diver, pole-vaulter and trampolinist are behind him.

In theory, the leaner you are, the greater your flexibility; the shorter you are, the less chance of getting your legs and feet tangled up in the parallel bars, the horse pommels, or each other. In other words, the less mass you have to haul around, the better. But these advantages of smallness can never be gained at the expense of strength. For along with flexibility, strength is the most important attribute a gymnast can possess. Here again, Thomas is well endowed.

"Kurt's strength-to-weight ratio goes right off the chart," says Tom Beach, a teammate of Thomas's at the 1976 Olympics. "He can bench press a hundred and eighty pounds, which is considerably more than he weighs. Even more amazing is to watch him do a series of pike presses on the parallel bars. A pike press is a strength move where you start from a handstand, lower your body down between the bars and then press back up to a handstand. They're real killers. I can do maybe four of them and I don't consider myself a weakling. But I stood there one day while Kurt did sixteen of them."

"I could probably do thirty right now if I had to," says Thomas, "but you can't be successful in this sport anymore just by being an animal. Twenty years ago, men's gymnastics was more of a muscle beach show. There was a lot of what I would call posing in floor exercise, mostly slow strength moves on parallel bars and nothing but crosses on rings. But now the emphasis has changed to much more swing, speed, action, and danger. It helps if you're strong enough to do thirty pike presses, but you also have to be supple enough to do sideways splits and mobile enough to perform a double back somersault and land safely on your feet."

The reason Thomas is so adept at carrying out these varied physical disciplines is that his body is a gymnast's dream, a collection of custom parts you have to order specially from gymnastics heaven. He has the face and hairdo of a Hardy Boy, which attracts a lot of young Thomas freaks to every meet and doesn't hurt him with the judges, either. Accented by a slim waist and

The Indiana State team giving a tumbling exhibition

The Japanese won five straight Olympic team titles (1960–64–68–72–76) and five straight World Championship team titles (1962–66–70–74–78).

Stretching out on parallel bars
Preparing for a dismount on pommel horse

no butt, his back and shoulders are so overdeveloped they make his chest look small. But for the purpose of moving his body up, down, and around during a routine, it is much better to have the bulk there than in front. Thomas also benefits from longish arms and short legs, a relationship which allows him to work much higher above the horse than most gymnasts and with less fear of snaring his legs in the pommels. This added height, or "amplitude" as judges refer to it, is one thing that separates his Thomas Flair from everyone else's. And in a sport that demands that the legs be kept straight and together nearly all the time, the shorter they are the easier that is to do.

Thomas's hands are the kind a person falling over a cliff would most like to be reaching for: big, strong, and meaty. They are so large, in fact, that they appear to have been grafted onto Thomas's wrists from a stevedore. This is a decided advantage when you're flying over the top of the high bar on a Veronin and need to grab hold again on the other side. More than their size, the consistency of Thomas's hands is what allows him to hit so many routines unerringly in a meet. The surface is extremely yellowed and sandpapery, but the palms are actually lumpy and pliable to the touch—like an old, beatup catcher's mitt, and just as dependable. Five years of three-a-day workouts have made these hands strong as a vise, and that is fortunate because the tension on the rings cables when a gymnast is at the bottom-most part of a giant swing has been measured at 1,200 pounds.

The style that emanates from this eclectic, but well integrated assortment of body parts is not only uniquely personal, but unique for an American—a combination of Russian recklessness and Japanese elegance. Thomas isn't as precise as the Japanese, but it wasn't easy learning the basics at Miami Central High School. Gymnasts were mentioned in the same breath with clarinet players and Hi-Y members, and Thomas admits he was distracted when the school's juvenile delinquents hurled boulders at the gym windows. Obviously, he

hasn't enjoyed the benefits of training in the Soviet Union, where they have deep, foam-padded tumbling pits that produce such Olympic floor-exercise champions as Nikolai Andrianov, who seem to work without fear. But Thomas isn't afraid of big tricks either—for instance, the 1½ twisting, 1¾ somersault he has been saving for Andrianov in Strasbourg. He can also change the pace of his floor-ex routine from fire to ice and back again so expertly that he appears to have memorized pages 58 and 59 of the judges' Code of Points, which deal with the concepts of *harmony, rhythm, tempo,* and *accent* in artistic gymnastics.

On one pass across the mat, Thomas is a runaway locomotive, ripping off multiple somersaults but landing so abruptly in a planned prone fall to his face that the crowd is left gasping long after he has stopped the action. Getting up on his hands, he twirls both legs above his head to prove that the Thomas Flair looks just as good on the floor-ex mat as it does on the horse. In fact, judges and fans seem to like it even better there. When Thomas needs a transition move to get himself out of a corner and on to his next pass, he doesn't merely turn around like most of his contemporaries. Risking disapproval from those judges who will die before they allow even a whiff of ballet in men's gymnastics, Thomas executes several light, pointed-toe kick steps and manages not to look like Olga or Nadia in the process. He has the sleekest looking strength move in the world—a press to a high V-seat—and his final pass is always full of fireworks. Everything in the routine is done in a crisp, nervy, cocksure manner that belies the difficulty of the movements.

"Kurt always looks like he's on the edge of catastrophe," says Tom Beach. "Which is the only way to score well if you're an American with no gymnastics heritage to give you clout with the judges. But in the heat of international competition, his approach still amazes me. It's like Leo Brouwer, the guitar player, says: When you're playing for yourself and there's nothing at stake, relax and give one hundred percent. But when

you play for other people, you need to hold something back. If you're good, eighty percent will be enough. Except that Kurt is too explosive ever to hold back."

One reporter was so impressed with Thomas's daring style and with the way he has elevated a cult sport into a new American art form, that she wrote: "He is men's gymnastics' Baryshnikov *and* its Balanchine."

The stage metaphor is a popular one. It also crops up in a remark made by Thomas's closest American pursuer, Bart Conner of the University of Oklahoma, who said: "Kurt has an actor's demeanor and a good stage feel for the sport. He can handle a greater degree of difficulty than the rest of us, and he really knows how to show off what he does best."

That such praise should come from Conner is ironic, since he covets Thomas's preeminent position in American gymnastics but at this point has yet to mount a serious challenge against him; a challenge Thomas desperately needs if he is to take on the world and win.

During an exhibition tour to the United States earlier in 1978, Andrianov, the reigning Olympic floor-ex, vault, rings, and All-Around champion, said he felt Thomas was fast becoming his most serious threat. But the reason Thomas's chances look bleaker than Gary Cooper's in *High Noon* is that the Russians and the Japanese are driven by a national obsession for gymnastics. This gives them a host of advantages over a lone American gunslinger.

The three countries couldn't be more different from one another in the way they treat gymnastics. While Americans are having their morning coffee with Gene Shalit and Erma Bombeck and wondering if the car will start, Moscow radio and TV are beginning their broadcast day with a hearty, 6:30 A.M. blast of "*Good morning, comrades! It is time for gymnastics class!*" The thud of feet hitting floor is so heavy they have to wear ear plugs over at the Kremlin. The same program is aired for the 7:00 and 8:00 shifts. And lest anyone's

joints get rusty, at 11:00 A.M. every day nine million Soviet factory workers stop whatever they're doing and engage in ten minutes of squat thrusts and leg lifts.

Mass calisthenics is no threat to Kurt Thomas. Only it says something about the Soviets' preoccupation with athletic development, a government-espoused mania that has a direct effect on the Russian gymnastics team. Mothers are told by the State that they must begin exercising their babies' limbs at birth. By the time children are nine years old in the Soviet Union they have been exposed to so much basic training in gymnastics that the future stars of the sport are already beginning to emerge. The cream of the crop is then shuttled off to government-subsidized sports academies, such as the Central Army Club, which has eighteen gymnasiums at its disposal and a staff of experienced coaches to run them. Once selected, few children lose interest or fail to give their all, because membership in these sports associations represents the best chance for the average Russian citizen to escape a lifetime of factory work. In that sense, he is no different from the poor American black kid who longs to escape his roots and make a million in the NBA. If it is a choice between operating a welding torch all your life or representing the Soviet Union in the glory of international athletic competition, there is no choice. To heighten the incentives still further, the tutelage young boys receive in these jock academies is not merely free. Parents of sports school pupils are paid as much as sixty rubles for every month their child is in training, two hundred if he wins a Soviet junior championship, five hundred for a senior title, and one thousand rubles—or fifteen hundred U.S. dollars—a month if he becomes an Olympic champion. In America, this kind of subsidy would make you ineligible; in the Soviet Union it puts you on Easy Street.

National talent hunts, organized training centers, State funding, and financial remuneration for parents of exceptional athletes—all these facets of the Soviet gymnastics machine are totally alien to the U.S.

method of producing an Olympic team. We just shake the tree every four years and wait to see who falls out.

Thomas is a prime example. He learned to walk by the age of seven months. In home movies taken by his mother when he was seven years old, Kurt does headstands, handstands, and plays the part of a tumbler in a neighborhood circus. Yet as talented as he was as a kid, Thomas didn't know gymnastics existed—and it never came looking for him. Instead of being pegged by the government for stardom at the age of nine, Kurt was messing around at Toby's Toy Store in Miami and trying to protect his lunch money from a band of grade school thugs. It wouldn't have mattered if he had been crazy about the sport, because his father died when he was young and there wasn't enough money for expensive lessons. Thomas stumbled into gymnastics by accident when, at fourteen, he wandered into a local junior college gymnasium and took a fancy to a man doing tricks on the high bar. For most of his success, he has only his perseverance and his God-given talent to thank.

As if Russian gymnasts didn't already have enough going for them, their coaches are getting some heavy assistance from Russian scientists. The standard method of analyzing a gymnast's routine in this country is with the naked eye. Thomas will make a pass across the floor-ex mat and Counsil will try to concentrate on the key parts, such as the mechanics of his somersaults. Then Counsil will stroll over to him and say something incisive, such as:

"I think you kicked out a little early."

To which Kurt may reply, "Oh, yeah? I know you're helping to rewrite the rulebook on vault and parallel bars, but how does that make you an expert on floor exercise!"

Everybody in the little gym has a good laugh and then Kurt goes back and tries the trick over again. They use the same trial-and-error method of training in the Soviet Union, except at the end of the day they can also check to see what the computer has to say

about it.

Soviet technology can break down a gymnast's routine into five hundred frames—or computer pictures —per second. This dwarfs the analytic capacity of ordinary 16 mm movie camera (twenty-four frames per second) and of motor-driven still cameras, which can deliver only five. The United States has access to the same kind of computers the Russians are using; what we don't have are the highly-trained biomechanical people they have hired to interpret all the additional information the computer can provide. Gymnastics, after all, is nothing more than simple physics and the computer can prepare printouts on everything from takeoff angles to escape velocities. To American ears, this may sound so advanced as to be irrelevant. But there are rumors that this kind of space-age technology has made it possible for the Russians to invent fifteen hundred new gymnastics tricks.

"I wouldn't be surprised," says Sadao Hamata, gymnastics coach at Stanford. "I know for a fact that some of the new moves we're seeing from the Russians are not man-made. I'm sure that in time a human being would have come up with the same moves on his own. But wouldn't it be nice to have a little computer around to help you think?"

Besides computer analysis, the Soviets employ another technique which sounds like it came straight from Dr. Frankenstein's laboratory: electrostimulation of muscles. By attaching a pair of electrodes to a bicep and shocking it with a mild electrical current (2,500 HTZ) for a series of ten-second intervals, Soviet doctors have been able to increase strength capacity in that muscle by as much as 40 percent in less than a month of treatments. When administered correctly, the procedure is practically painless and it can make a great deal of difference to a gymnast who is having trouble with pure strength moves, such as an iron cross on the rings. In other words, if you've got a big meet coming up, you just stop by the doctor's office once a day to get plugged in. Three weeks later, you're souped up

and ready to take on the world. The East Germans have even resorted to muscle biopsies in order to determine whether a young athlete has the type of "fast twitch" muscle that is conducive to good gymnastic skills. Anything the East Germans are doing has either been originated in, copied from, or discarded by the Soviet Union, so the Russians can't be strangers to muscle biopsies.

The Russian training pits are also something to see —100 feet long, 20 feet wide, eight feet deep, and filled to the brim with soft foam rubber. From a trampoline, the rings, or high bar, gymnasts can fly off in any direction going for as much height, distance, and air time as they can muster. Since the foam rubber pit cushions even the hardest landing, Russian gymnasts can eventually learn to control tricks that gymnasts from other countries can't even attempt for fear of serious injury.

The Soviets have tremendous scientific resources at their disposal and a penchant for gimmicks that can give them an edge—such as the foam-rubber training pit. But the reason they approach the sport in this manner has a lot to do with the fact that the Japanese have already cornered the market in matters of style and looking good. Their basic gymnastic skills are too fluid and technically perfect for words. So rather than trying to beat the Japanese at what they do best, the Russians have developed routines that are known as much for their risk and innovation as for their neglect of traditional form and beauty. The U.S. team calls Andrianov "a hucker," meaning he may not look graceful but he's athletic enough to do things that nobody else in the world can do. Andrianov is bow-legged, flaps his arms like a bird when he runs, and doesn't always stick his landings tight. But he was the first man in the world to perform a triple back somersault off the high bar in international competition, and he appears to be the wave of the future in men's gymnastics.

If the Russians' motto is "I can," then the Japanese creed is "I must," for nowhere in the world is gymnastics more of a religion than it is in Nippon. Baseball, golf, track and field, and skiing are also very popular, but none of those athletes show the kind of reverence for their sport that Japanese gymnasts do. They not only train all winter long in unheated gyms where gloves and heavy warmup suits are the order of the day, they seem to revel in it. They are impervious to pain, yet wouldn't dream of allowing someone to attach a pair of electrodes to their biceps. They believe that achievement flows from the heart, mind, and body —not through the wires of the latest electrostimulation machine—and that no sacrifice is too great if it brings one closer to perfection. In that sense, the Japanese behave more like a Samurai cult than a gymnastics team.

In Japan, college gymnasts live together in the same dormitory and are segregated according to a caste structure similar to that of the Samurai. The top ten athletes, as measured by their performance in competition, live in one dorm, while numbers eleven through fifty-five share more Spartan quarters. The lower-class gymnasts serve as errand boys for the first group, and seniority is always a rule of thumb. This is also evident in the coach-gymnast relationship, which operates on the same time-honored principles as that of father-son: When the older (and therefore wiser) man speaks, the younger man listens. He will do whatever he is told to do for as long as he is told to do it. This explains why the Japanese are thought to be so patient. They're not. Patience went out with the painting of screens. What the Japanese are is *obedient* and *dedicated*. This is what has made them rulers of men's gymnastics—over Russian science and everything else. •

"When I think back on my gymnastics training in Japan, I think of it as a way of life," says Mas Watanabe, a former Japanese national champion on high bar who is now program director for the United States Gymnastics Federation. "You have to understand that for three years, myself, eight other gymnasts, and a

coach lived together, studied together, and worked out together. One purpose. Nothing interfered. It was like a *kibbutz*."

The gymnast who will be remembered as personifying the Samurai ethic more than any other is Sawao Kato, the Japanese All-Arounder who refused to give in to serious injury, personal tragedy, or Father Time, and whose on-again, off-again reign as king of the sport produced more Olympic gold medals (eight) than any man had ever won before.

Always labeled "elegant" rather than "great" or "spectacular," Kato surprised his detractors by winning the Olympic All-Around at Mexico City in 1968. The crowd much preferred Mikhail Veronin of the Soviet Union and Akinori Nakayama of Japan, and Rex Bellamy of *The London Times* termed Kato's margin of victory (.25 of a point) an "arithmetic curiosity." Kato's consistency from event to event made him tough to beat in the All-Around, but the gymnasts' overall medal tallies in Mexico City seemed to justify the prevailing skepticism: Veronin (two gold, four silver, one bronze); Nakayama (three gold, two silver, one bronze); Kato (three gold, one bronze). Veronin and Nakayama performed much better in subsequent competition in the individual events and Bellamy seemed to be speaking for everyone when he wrote, "Kato will obviously have a lot of trouble confirming his new authority."

Kato did have a lot of trouble, though not for the reasons Bellamy surmised. He missed the 1970 World Championships because of a torn Achilles tendon, an injury that sidelines some athletes for life. He managed to recover in time for the 1972 Olympics in Munich, but was in no shape to win. He was bothered by a bad shoulder injured in a fall from the high bar and by a sore elbow that required a heavy bandage. He had not looked impressive at the Japanese Olympic trials, but then he never did.

Kato was the ultimate training freak, a man whose personal motto must have been, "Whatever it takes."

It wasn't unusual for him to spend 100 hours a month on a trick that was giving him problems, but he considered it a waste of time to work on things he did well. In the Olympic trials, his routines always included rough segments that other gymnasts would have edited out for the sake of vanity and a higher score. The Japanese are different in a lot of ways. Most countries pump their trials scores as high as possible in hopes of enhancing their reputation with the judges prior to the Games. But the Japanese are so notoriously strict in their national meet that their latest scores are always deceptively low around Olympics time. Opponents adjust their thinking accordingly. Sure enough, in Munich, Kato won the All-Around again, thanks to a 9.75 on his last exercise on high bar.

Just as he had four years earlier, Kato disappeared after the 1972 Olympics. An automobile accident in which a girl was killed and he was held accountable caused him to miss a year of training. When a series of injuries kept him out of the 1974 World Championships, all but his teammates figured he was through. Yet in Montreal, he was the Kato of old, rising Phoenix-like out of the ashes to win another gold medal. This time he didn't get it in the All-Around, losing out to Andrianov. But he did win the parallel bar competition, thereby becoming the first gymnast in history to win individual gold medals in three consecutive Olympics.

This is the heritage of success that Thomas must contend with when he takes on the Russians and the Japanese in France, and it is scarcely a thing of the past. Andrianov and his young teammate, Alexander Ditiatin, are the strongest one-two punch in men's gymnastics. And although Kato finally retired after Montreal at the age of twenty-nine, his successors—Kenmotsu, Kasamatsu, Kajiyama—make the Japanese the favorites in the team competition once again.

The gap in training is still a factor, too. Prior to the World Championships, the United States Gymnastics

Federation conducted only one training camp. *Only one?* The USGF was happy it could afford that one. The Japanese, on the other hand, have conducted six camps and the Russians more than that.

An American gymnast has never won a gold medal in the eighteen previous World Championships. Yet it seems the more obstacles that pile up against Thomas, the better he performs and the more apparent his eventual success becomes. There is a suspicion among teammates and opponents that he is bionic.

"The most amazing thing about Kurt is how fast he learns," says Counsil. "I guess it's because he's a true child of the Sixties; his method is all visual. He doesn't do too well when you try to teach a trick to him directly. He has to actually see another gymnast do it or watch it on videotape. Once he does, he usually has the move down in about fifteen minutes."

"I'll tell you how quick he is," says Mike Booth, a former ISU All-Arounder who is helping out in the gym while in graduate school. "I used to do the same 1½ twisting, 1¾ somersault that Kurt has been working on to take to Strasbourg. At least I tried to. For four months I did nothing but crash and burn on it. So one day I asked Kurt to take a look to see if he could tell what I was doing wrong. In four passes across the mat, he had it mastered. Not four months, mind you. *Four passes.* If it had been anyone else, I'd have been about half pissed. But with Kurt, you get used to that kind of thing."

Karl Schwenzfeier, the Montreal Olympic coach from Penn State, remembers Thomas watching videotapes of his teammates at the 1976 training camp: "Believe it or not, by the time camp was over, Thomas had sorted through everybody's routines, selected the tricks he liked best, and incorporated them into his repertoire. It was amazing. In fact, if he hadn't injured his finger a couple days before the start of the Games, he would have finished a lot higher than twenty-first in the All-Around."

"Gymnastics is moving so fast," says Thomas, "that the only way you get to be No. 1 is by always having something new to show the judges. You can't control what the other guys are going to do. So instead, you pile trick upon trick until the difficulty factor doesn't bother you. That doesn't mean you aren't scared the first time you try some of these tricks. But that's what practice is for—not only to help you learn a new move, but to take the thrill out of doing it.

"I go all out in a meet, but that's because I don't use anything that isn't absolutely locked in. In practice, I want to be as safe as possible. That means wearing the safety belt if I'm going up on high bar or rings. Or if I'm trying something difficult on parallel bars, floor, or vault, I make sure I've got a couple teammates or my coach around to catch me in case I'm about to land wrong. You have to have good spotters in this sport.

"Fear is the biggest problem a young gymnast faces, boys more so than girls. These young girls like Korbut and Comaneci aren't afraid of anything. They do whatever their coach tells them without hesitation. I guess that's because they're physically capable of doing incredible tricks long before they're emotionally equipped to realize how dangerous it all is. I've seen twelve-year-old girls do things in a big meet that I would hate to try in practice. And, while I'm twenty-two years old, I've stood on a lot of victory platforms with fifteen-year-old girls. The reverse is never true for little boys. At twelve, they can't do nearly as much as a little girl, and at fifteen they're still a long, long way from reaching their potential.

"It's odd, but girls' success in gymnastics often depends upon physical and emotional immaturity. As they grow up and develop women's bodies, they usually lose some of that precious flexibility and acquire other interests. At my age, most women gymnasts are washed up. Boys are just the opposite. They can't do great things until they begin to get strong and coordinated and until their confidence starts to flow. A man can remain at top form until he's thirty.

Each apparatus comes equipped with elements of danger peculiar only to it. High bar may be the most treacherous because of the tremendous speed and height that a gymnast achieves during his routine. As is the case on rings, a safety belt can dispel a lot of fears during practice.

The Thomas Flair gave Kurt a trademark and helped him establish a reputation in international gymnastic circles. It also looked good on TV. *(overleaf)*

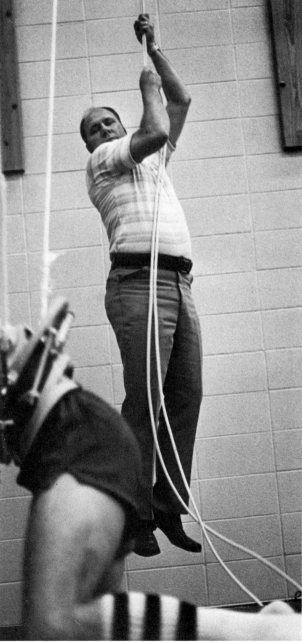

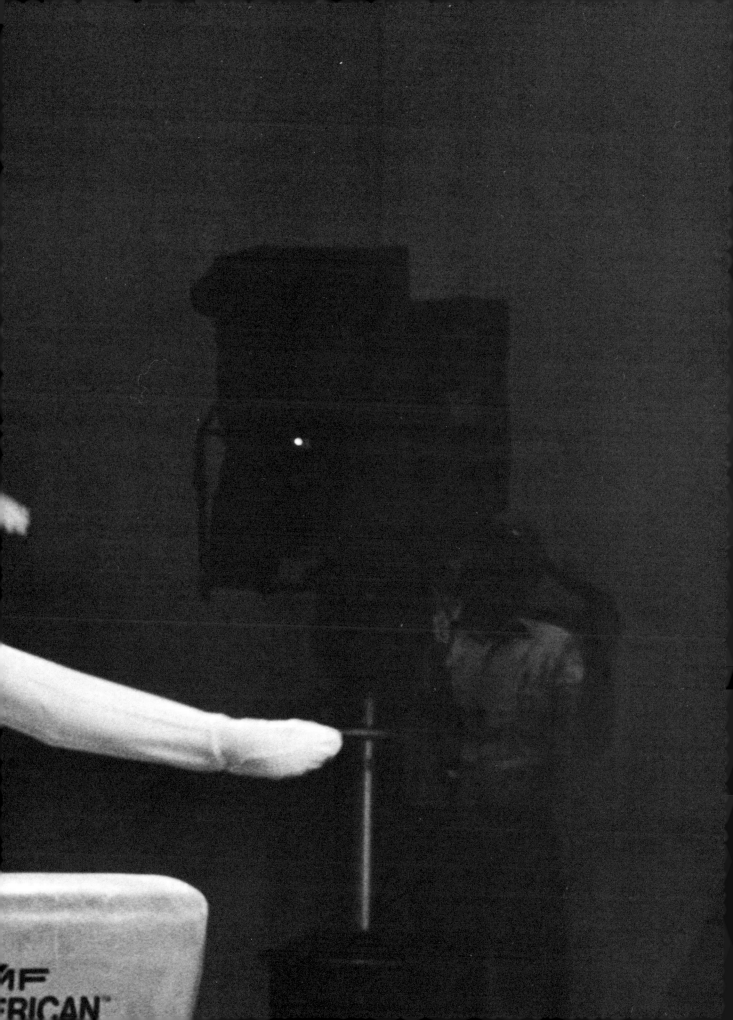

Mike Silverstein

"I didn't have any fear when I started out in gymnastics, and that was a definite asset. My coach said, 'Do anything.' And I pretty much did. But as soon as I got hurt for the first time, I started being afraid. Girls bounce back better. When I was a freshman at Indiana State, I learned how to do a double back somersault off the parallel bars. But I had never tried it at the end of a full parallel bars routine when I was tired. When Counsil said, 'Put it in,' I had nightmares about it for a week. But when I finally decided to try it, he was right there to spot me and I did it perfectly.

"Each event has its own peculiar dangers. High bar is probably the most treacherous because you're working eight to fourteen feet off the mat at high speed. Take the triple flyaway dismount I'm trying to perfect. This trick is scary—particularly if you think about it too much—and it isn't worth a damn if you can't land it right. Besides, you'd probably kill yourself. But you learn to build a triple flyaway in stages, just the way you would a house or a skyscraper. Once you've done two somersaults, it isn't too hard to hold on a little longer and go for three. You do have to try to *feel* three somersaults, however, because if you depend on your eyes to tell you where you are, all you see is a blur of walls, lights, and faces. Some gymnasts count to themselves, 'One . . . two . . . three,' in order to anticipate their landing. But over the years I seem to have acquired an air sense of where I am at all times during a trick."

Thomas has left one event out of his monologue on danger in gymnastics for the same reason he has left it for last in his workout: The pommel horse gives him very little trouble. To most of the world's gymnasts, this is his real badge of courage; while the horse ranks very low in potential danger, it leads the league in fear and loathing. When a gymnast botches up a big somersault on floor-ex and lands on his nose, he can at least count on a round of applause for the effort. But when a man falls off the pommel horse, the crowd merely groans. It's usually an awkward, slow-motion, you-can-see-it-coming-before-it-happens kind of fall, much like a hippo struggling to keep its fanny on the bank, but sliding back down into the muck instead.

Considering the altogether different manner in which he operates on the horse—pawing the air with his feet and riding high in the saddle—Thomas deserves his new trademark, the subsequent clout with international judges, and the talk show invitations. But Mike Silverstein's story is the opposite of Kurt Thomas's, and testimony to the fact that hard work and talent aren't always enough in this difficult and multifaceted sport. Silverstein is what you might call an "All-Arounder Minus One" in that he is a world-class gymnast in five events and a piece of hamburger on the horse. This has robbed him of a lot of rewards which seem right at his fingertips. Here are Silverstein's scores in the six events from the qualifying meet for the U.S. World Championship team:

	Floor Exercise	Rings	Vault	Parallel Bars	High Bar	Pommel Horse
Compulsories	9.25	9.45	9.25	9.35	9.25	7.0
Optionals	9.40	9.55	9.60	9.20	9.35	7.55

Silverstein's average for his five good events was 9.35, better than all but three men in the sixteen-man field. Unfortunately for him, that's not the way international teams are chosen. Counting the pommel-horse event, Silverstein finished eleventh and only seven men—six regulars and one alternate—will make the trip to France. If he had averaged merely 8.2 on horse, he would have edged Minnesota's Tim LaFleur for the alternate spot. The only problem with that analysis is that Silverstein's collegiate *best* is 7.95. In the 1978 USGF Championships, he scored a 4.55, falling off the apparatus four or five times and eroding any confidence he had built up during his senior year at Temple.

"The pommel horse stands apart from the rest of my personality," says Silverstein, who is now enrolled

in the Temple law school, "and I'm not going to pretend that it doesn't bother me. In school, I feel I have unlimited potential, my social life is well adjusted, and on the other five events I'm fine. On horse, somehow it's different. My coach thinks that most of my problem is physical; I don't have the amount of shoulder support strength that I should. But the closer I get to international teams without making them, the more psychological problems I have to deal with. Sometimes I dread going out there and making a fool of myself, and when I come back I'm saying to myself, 'How come everybody else can get through it and I can't?'

"Nobody in the sport is malicious about it, but in trying to make me feel better they all end up saying the same thing, 'Do you know you're good enough in the other five events to win medals overseas?' Yes, I realize that. And I also realize that unless I improve, I'm no closer to being an All-Arounder than a pommel-horse specialist is."

It is after six o'clock when Thomas finishes his brief run-through on the horse, and he is tired. As he heads down the hall for his nightly sauna (you wonder why anyone would bother after three hours in the ISU gym), a reporter who has been sitting throughout the entire workout kicks off his shoes and prepares to do what he has done many times at college basketball practices—show what he can do. In no time he has made the rounds of all the apparatus and arrived back at his shoes. This isn't basketball practice. He can't do a thing.

The Merv Griffin show that evening is a lukewarm affair until Kurt is introduced. He does his Flair perfectly and easily outshines an all-star cast of Dick Clark, George Gobel, and Walter Cronkite's daughter, Kathy. Near the end of their conversation, Merv notices Kurt's hands and the camera zeroes in to give America a closer look. Merv says:

"You could put a cigarette out in your palm and not even feel it!"

Dick Clark is amazed. But not as much as the two New York City mounted policemen who wandered into an American Cup workout at Madison Square Garden one time when Thomas was whipping around the high bar.

"You believe that guy?" said Officer Werbacher.

"Nope," said Officer Dabenigno. "I'd rather be doing what we're doing."

The Gymnast

Gymnasts are an extremely obscure and rarefied breed of athlete, owing mainly to the fact that gymnastics is such a self-defeating enterprise you can't even be *bad* at it in the beginning. God did not think it wise for man to be flinging his body about in such acrobatic fashion, so He made sure it would take so long to learn important moves—five years was His recommendation for a "peach basket" on parallel bars—that only the strongest, most obstinate individuals would ultimately make the grade. He had originally intended for Jimmy Connors and Pete Rose to become gymnasts, but they were lured away, as most young boys are, by the comparative ease with which they could get started in other sports.

The beauty of tennis or baseball is that even a complete novice can approximate the skills of the sport's most talented practitioners. A wild-swinging six-year-old can knock a tennis ball past his dad every once in a while, and the callowest Little Leaguer will sometimes surprise you by picking up a grounder and throwing to second base for the force out. This is called instant gratification and it's what keeps a young Connors or Rose coming back for more. Too bad it's such an unknown element in men's gymnastics. Not only are the movements so painstakingly difficult they have to be learned by increments, they are for the most part wholly unnatural.

The difference between gymnastics and football—or most any other sport you want to compare it to—is that gymnastics demands the mastering of so much more technique before an athlete really gains *the knack*. Certainly a halfback must be more than big and fleet afoot; he must be able to memorize his playbook, withstand tremendous physical punishment, and hang onto the football. However, his main task, as Vince Lombardi once outlined it, is to "run to daylight." Exiting the high bar with a full-twisting double back somersault is something more.

Considering the arsenal of sophisticated skills that world-class gymnasts must exhibit, it is something of a paradox that most of them are dropouts who couldn't make it in other sports.

"I don't know many gymnasts who started out with the idea of becoming a star in this sport," says Jay Whelan, a coach at North Carolina State who narrowly missed making the 1978 World Championship team. "It's usually a case of, 'Hey, here is something I can actually *do* for a change!' In this society, it is smart for a man who isn't going to be a doctor or lawyer to pick a sport where he might earn some financial rewards later on. But being small usually takes that choice away from you. You're overlooked by coaches, discouraged by friends, or just plain not good enough to compete in the prestige sports. Gymnastics opened up a whole new world for me. True, I have to do my pliés every day—which some guys think is funny. But I've learned to do flips and now people want to watch *me* perform. That's a terrific kick!"

Whelan's experience is typical. It was the same for Thomas, who, at thirteen, was still trying to be a football player. Except he was such a runt he was able to talk his way onto a Tiny Tot team for ten-year-olds. It was the same for talk show host Dick Cavett, another short person who wasn't much of an all-around athlete as a kid growing up in Lincoln, Nebraska, but who found solace as a pommel horse specialist.

"Being a member of the L-Club at Lincoln High was a pretty important social item, and at that point in my life all I could think about was winning my letter," Cavett recalls. "I had been told by coaches that major sports were out for me due to my size. So I decided to try the horse, mainly because it was the only piece of gymnastic equipment the school had. For some reason, probably *because* of my size, I was good at it. In fact, I was Nebraska state champion my sophomore and junior years. That got me into the L-Club and I will never forget what my coach said as I walked up on stage to receive my letter: 'This goes to Dick Cavett, for side-horse work *par excellence*.' I still consider it one of the high points in my life."

Bart Conner

Having recovered from an operation to repair the broken vertebrae in his neck, Henry Boerio of France deserves congratulations.

Perhaps it is these shared experiences of early ineptitude and subsequent success which account for the clear-headed insight that most gymnasts have into themselves. They are not as voluble as some of the pop psychology nuts you find in track and field. But they have a lot on their minds and—never having been covered by the American press—a lot to say. Pose the question to Thomas, "What are gymnasts really like?" and he responds as though he has been waiting years for someone to ask.

"Gymnasts are quick mentally; they have to be because it takes brains as well as physical talent to learn these tricks and then carry them out in competition. When I'm really cooking on horse, it may look like my body is doing all the work and I'm just along for the ride. Uh-uh. My head is still pushing all the buttons. It's when your mind and body don't work together that you get into trouble. At the World Championship qualifying meet in Oklahoma City, I was on the way to what could have been a 9.9 or even a 10.0 routine in floor exercise when, all of a sudden, I landed in a heap. In practice that day I had decided to change my third pass across the mat to a roundoff [cartwheel], a flip-flop [back handspring], and a double full [back somersault with two twists]. But apparently I hadn't thought about it enough before the meet that night. My body was used to doing the old sequence without the flip-flop. So when my mind went to sleep in the middle of the routine, that's what my body tried to do—leave out the flip-flop. By the time I realized what was wrong, it was too late to do anything but fall. I had to settle for a 9.4.

"I think a lot of people come to gymnastics meets for the same reason they go to the Indy 500: to see exciting, difficult maneuvers and—if they're lucky—to see somebody like me crack up. I don't mean they're *hoping* I will, just that the possibility intrigues them. These same people, by virtue of the tricks they see us do, probably think gymnasts are immune to fear. They're wrong; we're all human, and anyone who was

in Oklahoma City the night the men's team sat in the stands watching the women's competition saw the proof. I don't know what went wrong, but it was an extremely bad night for the women. Some of the young girls were trying things they obviously couldn't handle, because bodies were flying everywhere. It's a miracle someone wasn't hurt badly. I thought one girl had broken her neck during floor exercise and another girl missed a flip on balance beam and really landed badly. It was an awful scene, as you could tell by looking at us guys in the stands. Bart Conner had his hands over his eyes, I had my warmup jacket stuffed in my mouth, and when things really started to get out of hand, several guys were too scared to watch any more. They actually got up and left the arena. When it's not you in control, and you're not sure whether the person down on the floor knows what he or she is doing, that's when gymnastics seems really hairy.

"Another misconception about gymnasts is that we're the best conditioned athletes in the world. I happen to think we're the most talented, but when you say 'best conditioned' it depends on what you mean. I was looking through a couple of books in Coach Counsil's office the other day and I came across some statistics on how well various kinds of athletes do in cardiovascular tests. Being a health education major at Indiana State, I know a little bit about this area, at least enough to know that 'cardiovascular uptake' refers to the amount of oxygen that a person can take in and distribute to all parts of his body. These kinds of tests are considered an accurate index of how in-shape you are. The higher your score, the better able you are to sustain and recover from prolonged physical activity. Anyway, according to this one book, researchers tested the cardiovascular uptake of two hundred and ninety-one Japanese athletes who were trying out for the Japanese Olympic team. Of the nineteen sports represented, marathon runners scored the highest, followed by basketball players and swimmers. Gymnasts—*Japanese gymnasts*, mind you, the

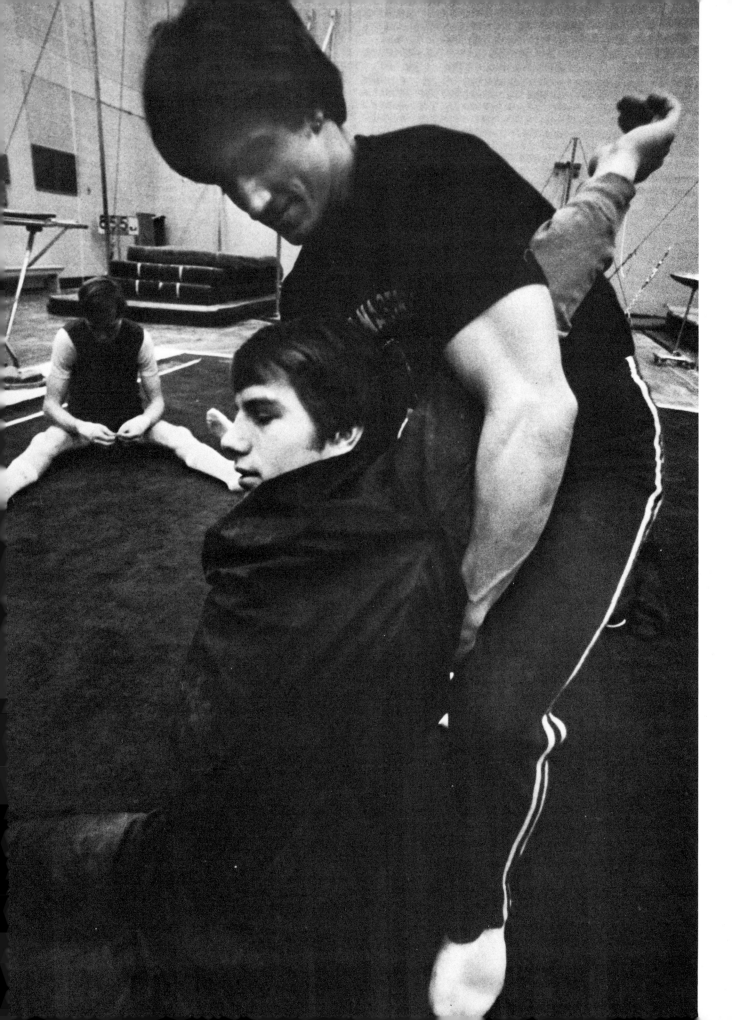

best in the world—were way down in sixteenth place. The only athletes they beat were equestrians, yachtsmen, and marksmen, none of whom do much under their own power. This doesn't surprise me, however, because gymnastics requires only short bursts of physical activity where cardiovascular uptake isn't such an important factor. Floor exercise takes a minute, the vault about five seconds, and the other four events maybe forty seconds each. And there's always time to recover; I can't ever remember feeling tired and unable to do my best just because it was the last event of the evening. Cardiovascular training might help you over the course of a week-long competition like the World Championships, but I'd rather spend forty-five minutes working on tricks than running five miles. Besides, I die of boredom after two.

"Gymnasts are very superstitious—I knew a guy who had to click his heels together twice before he would mount the pommel horse—yet they do not believe in luck. In baseball, you can check your swing and bloop a double over the first baseman's head and it's just as good as blasting one off the wall. Not in gymnastics it wouldn't be! Every little movement you make is being critiqued against a judge's mental picture of perfection. Every little mistake, whether it's a wobble, a loss of balance, or just some motion that doesn't look aesthetic, costs you points.

"To keep themselves in the proper frame of mind to handle this constant pressure, gymnasts usually project bright, fresh attitudes—like they're high on life. I think this stems from the fact that gymnastics is essentially a one-man sport. We may keep score by teams at the NCAAs or by countries at the World Championships, but the whole thing boils down to a very private, inner competition with yourself. The only way to succeed is to train hard and try to build up as much self-confidence as possible. To do that, you must stay motivated and never get down on yourself. That brings us back to the bright, fresh attitude thing again.

"Athletes who compete in team sports have to do everything in groups, to the point where you wonder whether they can take care of themselves when they're left alone. They are driven to airports, taxied to hotels, led to dinner, bed-checked for curfew violations, bussed to arenas, helped through school, and shielded from the press when they don't want to talk. Gymnasts are much more independent, again because they have to be. I've flown halfway around the world by myself, attended meets in Europe without my coach, changed clothes in foreign cabs when I was late to a competition and didn't think I'd have time to find the locker room, worked out morning and night on my own for five years, and so on. You learn to depend on yourself in critical situations; that's one of the bonuses of competing in a so-called minor sport.

"When was the last time you saw an ugly gymnast? I *never* have. They all have sleek, lean, tight bodies— the kind that look like they can do *anything*—a decent face, and a neat overall appearance. That's what sells best with the judges. Everyone's hair is cut short, as much for neatness as to keep it out of their eyes, and you won't see many beards or moustaches. Zoltan Magyar, the Hungarian pommel horse expert, sometimes wears a moustache and lets his hair get shaggy. Counsil is convinced it's hurting him with the judges, but you wouldn't know it from looking at his scores."

As immaculately enticing as these tight, lean, well-sculptured bodies may look to judges, fans, and the people inside them, sexual activity between gymnasts is practically nil. For one thing, nobody has the time. "Where can you take a girl who spends every minute of the day either training, studying, or sleeping?" says Thomas. "A guy might say to a girl, 'Hey, I'm going to the Chunichi Cup in Japan next month. Are you?' That's a typical date between gymnasts." For another thing, most of the women gymnasts are really just girls and far too young to go out with their counterparts on the men's side. While age and lack of time contribute to this particular kind of celibacy, the greatest factor

Special shoes allow a gymnast to flex his foot while maintaining proper traction; in socks you slip and slide, in bare feet you stick to the mat.

is the suppression of a normal feminine sex drive—for which some women's coaches are only too willing to take credit. One of them is Muriel Grossfeld, a former Olympian and Olympic coach who runs a live-in school for gymnastics in Milford, Connecticut. In *Penthouse* magazine, Grossfeld was quoted as saying:

"I've worked damned hard at keeping these girls in line so that they can become champs. I've conditioned them to think I can see *anything* they're up to, whether or not they're in the gym. And it's working! They've got to reach the point where all they think about in their lives is being the best in the gym. Nothing else matters. We give 'em so much to do that they don't have time for boys. That would kill everything. Some of my girls start to date, but we uncover their suitors and offer some 'friendly discouragement.' Sex hardly ever comes up in my discussions with the girls, but when it does, I tell them to absolutely abstain. And I'm sure as hell not about to allow them to take birth control pills. Sex, I tell them, will only slow them down, and we don't have time for girls who allow themselves to get mowed over by a guy. No way."

When a *Sports Illustrated* writer went to interview American ballet dancer Edward Villella a few years ago, the two men had scarcely shaken hands when Villella said, "I know the question you're dying to ask even before you ask it: Am I straight?" The same question persists about male gymnasts—not because they have given up trying to get female gymnasts into bed, but because, as Jay Whelan says, some people do not consider pliés a proper exercise for a red-blooded American male, and they are uncomfortable with other accouterments of the sport.

"I have never been asked flat-out if I'm gay," says Thomas. "Maybe because I'm married. But I get similar questions, like 'Why do you wear those white tights?' or 'Can I see your ballet shoes?' I guess some people just can't relate to an athlete who doesn't wear a helmet and cleats. To begin with, we don't wear tights. These things I've got on are more like light-weight ski pants. The reason they're white is because that color gives you a clean, streamlined look that sells best with the judges. I call the shoes 'slippers,' but I guess they really aren't too different from men's ballet shoes. The main thing is that they allow you to flex your foot. Just wearing socks doesn't work because your feet slip and slide. If you went barefoot, your feet would perspire and stick to the mat. I've also been told I stand and walk like a ballet dancer—you know, with my toes pointed out and my heels together. I've never taken any dance lessons, but Bart and some of the other guys have and I'm told this is the same as 'first position' in ballet. Gymnasts use it because they're taught to land that way, rather than with both feet right together. The wider the stance, the greater chance of what we call 'sticking your dismount'—that is, of landing stock-still with no hops or shuffling of the feet afterward.

"To enjoy men's gymnastics to the fullest, the public is going to have to accept the sport for what it is: unique, exciting, and totally different from Monday Night Football. Gymnasts have to behave differently than football players. Look at these hands of mine; they're the most overused part of my body. If I don't want them to crack open and bleed from six hours of working out every day, guess what I have to do every night? Put cold cream on them and wear gloves to bed. And if I've got a big meet coming up like the World Championships, I ask Beth to let me do the dishes all week. It helps keep my hands soft. Now if any of this gets out, we'll all be locked up.

"At Indiana State, people are always sticking their heads in the doorway of the little gym while the guys on the team are taking care of each other, and I know what some of them must be thinking: *Look at those guys, they have to be queer!* When I say 'taking care of each other,' I mean it's a lot easier to get loose if another guy rubs the bottom of your feet or cracks your back for you. I can't help it if it sounds weird, it's gotta be done. And just like when you've got a bad

itch, it's always better if somebody else scratches it for you. The guy who takes care of me is Lee Battaglia, an All-Arounder from outside Chicago. If you look in on us every day at three-thirty, you'll find me stretched out on my stomach with Lee sitting on my butt, either kneading the soles of my feet or rubbing my back. It's an automatic ritual by now; we don't even talk to each other. I'm probably thinking about Beth or planning my workout. In return for all the effort he puts in, Lee gets a set of warmups from the Chunichi Cup or a gym bag from the Romanian Invitational or whatever I bring back from international meets during the year."

It isn't surprising that the average American sports fan would question the maleness of men's gymnastics. Not only does it have some unusual trappings, its coaches and administrators have never been sure how to sell the sport. Should they be playing Madison Square Garden, Lincoln Center, or the Big Top?

"I'm probably overly sensitive to questions in this area," says Roger Counsil, "but our biggest problem in getting men's gymnastics to grow has been our inability to break down the Gladiator Syndrome in this country. Until Kurt began to hit it big, it was simply not a prestige thing for a little boy to be taking up gymnastics. And even now, if you check out the packs of kids trying to get Kurt's autograph at a meet, seventy-five percent of them are young girls. The number of gymnasts in the United States has jumped from forty thousand in 1970 to five hundred thousand today, but again seventy-five percent of them are girls. Olga Korbut started the fad at the 1972 Olympics and when Nadia Comaneci racked up all those 10.0s in Montreal in 1976, it blossomed into a movement.

"Women's gymnastics seems to profit a great deal from the use of music and choreography in floor exercise. It's a real crowd pleaser. But I'll be damned if I want Kurt to go strutting around the mat like José Greco; I don't like that ballet garbage he does in the corners, as it is. That's what I mean about being ultrasensitive. On the other hand, a lot of international meets I go to just seem dead without some kind of noise to support the gymnasts. As a compromise, a lot of colleges have begun using background music to liven up their meets. Nobody is choreographing any routines to it, and I don't see what's wrong with creating a little *Saturday Night Fever* atmosphere if it brings people into the arena and helps them enjoy the sport. But so far the Federation Internationale de Gymnastique has voted down all resolutions that seek to incorporate music into men's gymnastics. The FIG delegates are definitely afraid of it.

"I'm not sure how gymnastics came to be considered a sissy sport or how people can go on believing that—even if they've only watched it on television. Ted Williams always maintained that hitting a baseball thrown at a hundred miles an hour was the most difficult task in the world of sports. But surely even Ted Williams would admit that the consequences of swinging and missing a baseball are less dire than missing your dismount on high bar. I'll never forget when Roberto Richards, a Cuban gymnast, landed wrong coming off the high bar during team competition in Montreal. There wasn't much doubt he had broken his leg because you could hear the bone snap all over the arena. That ought to be macho enough, or do we have to put a hammer lock on each other? Nobody laughs at wrestlers' tights."

As the standard-bearer for a sport proud of its elegance and daring but concerned about its virility, Kurt Thomas could hardly be better suited. He is as pert as a young man can be, he has as much panache as Olga or Nadia, and yet he would just as soon punch you in the nose as be called "effeminate."

The word for Thomas's appeal is *androgynous*, and it's a phenomenon whose time has come—and not just in gymnastics. Long before John Wayne's death, American audiences had developed a taste for softer, more subtly compelling European-style heroes, among them Mick Jagger and Rod Stewart, John Curry

and Toller Cranston, Rudolf Nureyev and Mikhail Baryshnikov, Bjorn Borg and Guillermo Vilas. And while American boys haven't exactly flocked to gymnastics in hopes of emulating Thomas's refreshing new image, there is a good chance they will. Everyone loves a champion, and as Roger Counsil says, "When it comes to winning, Kurt has tunnel vision."

As a freshman at Indiana State, Thomas was so cocky ("Obnoxious and impossible to live with," is his own description) that several seniors on the team wanted to tell him off. But he was already a 55.0 All-Arounder and that was something to be cocky about. Thomas had other reasons. As he was growing up in Miami, his apartment complex—with its four swimming pools—was gradually becoming an island in the middle of a black ghetto. To stay out of the intensive care ward, he had to learn some guerrilla warfare tactics.

"I never really liked to fight," says Thomas, "but a lot of times I didn't have any choice. So I'd always throw the first punch and hope there was somebody around to break it up quick. Right in front of the principal's office was a good spot, much better than in some alley. My problem was being small and always getting picked on. But after a while that stuff started to motivate me, and I think it carries over to my career in gymnastics. It's really true what they say about short people: *They want to feel powerful.* At least I do. Why else would I have gotten a big Doberman when the trailer I live in is barely big enough for my wife and me? Because I think mean dogs with big chests are cool. Don't you think it's neat to have a dog that people are afraid of! You gotta understand that I was the one who was always afraid as a kid. I even hired my sister to help me run my paper route because I was scared some big dude was going to come along at four A.M. and rip me off. What I thought my sister was going to do about it, I don't know. But it felt good to have her there.

"I remember two stories about growing up in a bad neighborhood. One morning I was folding my papers when I saw some derelict breaking into the local liquor store. My sister wouldn't get out of bed that day, so I had to call the owner myself. He called the cops, they caught the thief, and I got a fifty-dollar savings bond as a reward. I was a hero! Then there was the time I was working at McDonald's and a strange-looking guy came in just before closing. I was sweeping up over in the corner, but I could tell by the way he was hassling this girl at the counter that he was stone drunk. When he really started giving the girl a hard time, I went over and threw a wild punch at him. He took it right on the chin and was unconscious when he hit the floor. When I think about it now, I realize what a crazy thing it was to do. The guy could have stuck a knife in my ribs. But I was taking karate at the time and I probably thought I was Bruce Lee. When the police arrived, they said, 'All right, who slugged this guy?' I told them I did, but that he had been asking for it. They took a good look at me—I was about five-foot-three then and maybe a hundred and fifteen pounds—and just laughed. They never did believe that I knocked the guy out. Of course, I was afraid he would come back and kill me when he woke up, so I quit the job and never went back."

Thomas's candid reflections on his dark past probably seem scandalous to those bright, fresh, high-on-life types who are so predominant in gymnastics. What, then, would they think if they found out he was once a petty thief and that he knew guys in high school who got their kicks by sniffing transmission fluid? "They'd never believe it," laughs Thomas. "It even sounds wild to me now."

Thomas is not wild anymore, but he will consent to an occasional beer to help him unwind after his evening workout. Nor is he obnoxious and impossible to live with, as Beth can attest. He can be a bit abrasive, or the most polite Kiwanis Club speaker you can imagine. Even his closest rival, Bart Conner, has complimented him on how he has managed to mature

amid so much success.

"Kurt knows he's good," says Conner, "but I think he's handling himself pretty well for a guy who is appearing on talk shows and all. He knows how to work hard and he's not going to let himself drift just because he's been on TV. Most of the guys I know like and respect him."

Thomas's relationship with Conner says as much about his personality as anything else. He genuinely likes Bart, and when the situation is a noncompetitive one, he acts accordingly. But Kurt is also desperately afraid of not being the best, and Bart is easily good enough to reawaken that fear in him every time they compete—whether it's Indiana State vs. Oklahoma or even when he and Bart are on the same side, as they will be when they represent the United States in Strasbourg. The Japanese have told Thomas that he is fortunate to have Conner around. They feel he needs four or five more Conners to contend with before the internal competition in the United States can begin to make up for the head start that Japan and the Soviet Union have in men's gymnastics. This explains why Kurt's principal preoccupation at the World Championships will be thinking to himself: *Gotta beat Bart, gotta beat Bart.* Conner is his foil, and despite protestations to the contrary, Bart would dearly love to be in Kurt's slippers.

"I think it's important to have the Olga Korbuts, the Nadia Comanecis, and the Kurt Thomases," says Conner. "But what Kurt is doing now is building a Bruce Jenner image. And I don't believe in the media setting goals for people. I know where I stand in world gymnastics right now and I like my position."

Given the fact that their bodies are so similar, and that they are both obsessed by the same goal, Thomas and Conner could scarcely be more dissimilar.

Kurt is brown-haired and brown-eyed; Bart is blond-haired and green-eyed. Kurt's father died when he was seven; Bart's dad, a structural engineer in Morton Grove, Illinois, was a guiding force throughout his son's

early training. Bart's style is clean and efficient, just what you might expect from someone whose dad used to work for the aerospace industry; Kurt looks like he was trained by Bruce Lee. In deference to the judges, both demonstrate polite refinement during a meet. But Bart is merely being himself, while Kurt is a boy behaving himself in church. When Bart finishes a routine, his smile is the definitive cute and his message to the judges is unmistakable: *Aren't I something!* Kurt's smile isn't nearly as toothy, and his raised fists seem directed more at his opponents. His message is also unmistakable: *Take that, you turkey!*

These same distinctions have existed between them for nearly a decade, ever since the Juniors competition during high school days when Bart, not Kurt, always won. In fact, there was a time when Conner was expected to lead the United States out of the gymnastics Dark Ages, but Kurt overtook him in college. Both gymnasts seemed comfortable with their symbiotic relationship. But thanks to an injudicious comment by Bart's coach at Oklahoma, Paul Ziert, a minifeud has begun to brew.

The trouble started at the 1978 NCAA championships, where Oklahoma won the team championship and Conner the All-Around. The task was made easier by the fact that Thomas had excused himself from the year's college competition in order to test the international waters. A year earlier, at the 1977 NCAAs, Indiana State and Oklahoma had tied for the team title and Kurt had easily beaten Bart in the All-Around. But with Thomas busy winning the 1978 Champions All meet in London and the Romanian Invitational in Bacau, Conner became the class of the States. Keyed to a fever pitch by the Sooners' NCAA sweep, Ziert told reporters that he was especially proud of his kind of gymnasts.

"What kind is that?" asked the press.

"We don't have any *plumbers* at Oklahoma," Ziert replied.

"What is a plumber?"

"A plumber is a guy who just tries to *get through* his routines. We also call it the GT-Method. It's a typical American gymnastics attitude, and it means the guy will probably be happy getting 8.95s for the rest of his life."

Ziert's remarks implied that everybody else had plumbers but him, and such haughtiness was not well received by his fellow coaches. Counsil, in particular, wondered whether Ziert would have been in position to make any speeches had Thomas been in the field.

Then, too, there was the flap over Kurt's Dial soap commercial. Having underwritten the USGF's operating expenses for two years to the tune of $1.25 million, the Armour-Dial Corporation was anxious to get Thomas on-camera pushing Dial soap. "We wanted to sponsor a sport that was *sweaty*, but *clean-cut*," said Joel Hobbs of Dial, "and Kurt certainly brings out that aspect of men's gymnastics." Since NCAA regulations prohibit a college athlete from using his name to sell a product, it was agreed by the NCAA, the USGF, and Dial that Kurt could appear in the commercial—just not by name. He would be the sweaty, but clean-cut young man doing the Thomas Flair on the horse and then enjoying an invigorating Dial soap shower afterward. A film crew from New York flew to Oklahoma City and on the morning after the World Championship qualifying meet, they began shooting two sixty-second commercial spots with Kurt.

Thomas was full of bluster, having fallen during his floor-ex routine the previous evening and done no better than a tie for first place with Bart. When the director of the crew said, "Okay, would you step up to the bar?" Kurt coldly corrected him. "It's called a horse, you know." Naturally, as interested as he is in Kurt's fame, Conner was not far away. About seventy-five extras were needed to simulate a cheering crowd, and so Bart volunteered to do for TV what he sometimes finds hard to do in real life: cheer for Kurt. The shooting took most of the day and all seemed to go well with Kurt,

the crew, and the crowd. But the commercial was later scrapped because three college coaches complained to the NCAA that this kind of thing was improper. Their identities were never revealed, but Thomas and Counsil suspect that Paul Ziert was one of them.

"People are always asking me about the plumbers thing," says Bart, "just like they're always asking me when I'm going to beat Kurt. I prefer not to worry about either one of them. The plumbers thing was supposed to stay within our team, something to motivate us. And when I'm ready to beat Kurt, I will. I do think it's wise for me to keep a little distance from him right now and concentrate on my own gymnastics, because a couple times when we've been out on the floor at the same time—say, me on rings and Kurt on horse—I've found myself *caring* a lot about the quality of his performance. Well, as soon as you start worrying about the other guy's routines, that's when the apparatus starts to bite back. Really, it's like they have a life of their own. Sometimes after a workout I'll walk back into the gym when the lights are out and get amazed by the whole thing. I'm never that startled by anything I do in gymnastics, but with the lights off, those contraptions are really weird-looking—like some implements of torture. That's when I say to myself: *Who do you think you are, and what are you doing in this place?*"

In ninth grade at Miami Central High School, Thomas was already capable of holding an L-support, a stepping stone to the more difficult L-cross where the gymnast's arms extend straight out from the body.

Kurt's Story

When Eleanore Thomas's youngest son, Kurt, was nine years old, she took him to see a genetic specialist at Miami's Jackson Memorial Hospital because, as she recalls, "The poor little thing was so tiny, I mean just *bones*, that I was afraid he'd die if he lost five pounds. I was sure he was going to be a midget."

X-rays of Kurt's hands confirmed that his growth was retarded by at least a year, and further examination revealed not one but two heart murmurs. The doctors adopted a wait-and-see attitude, telling Mrs. Thomas they would have to keep a close watch on Kurt for the next five years to see how he developed.

Not very much, was the answer. By 1970, the heart murmurs had gone away, but at the age of fourteen Kurt was one of the smallest freshmen—four-foot-nine and seventy-seven pounds—to register for classes at Miami Central High School. He was a tough kid, nonetheless, and a pretty good athlete for his size. When he returned to Jackson Memorial for his final checkup, Dr. William Cleveland had looked him over and told his mother he would probably turn out fine. Not big, she was to understand, since she was barely five feet tall and her late husband had been only five-foot-six. But Kurt could expect to lead a normal life.

Thomas took his first steps toward disproving that "normal life" prognosis when he wandered into a gymnastics workout at Miami-Dade Junior College a few days before the start of the fall semester at Miami Central. "I looked up and saw this guy swinging on the high bar," Kurt recalls. "He wasn't a whole lot bigger than I was, and he made it look like a neat sport. That's how I happened to go out for gymnastics." Unbeknownst to little Kurt, Miami Central High School had never had a gymnastics team before—nor does it have one today. But ah, the hand of fate. In 1970, someone had just decided to start one.

Thomas may not have looked like world-champion material when he walked into the Miami Central gym and asked for a tryout, but neither was Don Gutzler much of a gymnastics coach. He hadn't grown his beard yet, but he did have a moustache, a generous shock of black hair, and the droll smile of your basic, hippy-dippy ex-jock. He was only twenty-three years old and had taught physical education in junior high school the year before. Yet somehow he had managed to talk the Miami Central administrators into adding a gymnastics team over the protestations of the athletic director, who offered to raise Gutzler's salary a thousand dollars if he would forget the whole thing and just teach phys ed.

"I'll admit it wasn't much of an idea on paper," says Gutzler. "Gymnastics has always been an elite sport for upper-middle-class kids. Here we were at Miami Central, right on the edge of the ghetto with lots of junkies hanging around, numerous assaults, and characters walking into school from off the street who had no business being there. Still, I had a hunch we could make it go. I told the kids in my first-day phys ed classes that if they were interested in gymnastics, they should meet with me after school. I think maybe ten showed up. Kurt was one of them and I can still remember how he looked. He was wearing a pair of oversized shorts from the Army-Navy surplus store and sporting a pair of stringbean arms that could scarcely have held up a violin. He looked up at me and said, 'Do you think I could be a gymnast?' Like his mom always says, he was so *cute*. But he didn't look like any kind of athlete. This was my first stab at coaching gymnastics and I didn't know what to look for, so I said to him, 'You're so skinny you're going to have to build up a lot of muscle.'"

"Gutz thought big guys would make the best gymnasts because that's the way it looked to him in the magazines," says Kurt. "He doesn't remember this, but that first day he kind of gave me the brush-off, told me to come back next week. Meanwhile, he had told the bigger guys to report for practice on Monday. Luckily, I found out about it and showed up too. It wasn't long before he found out those other guys couldn't do handstands. I'd been doing them on the playground

After finishing last at the Junior Olympics the previous year, Thomas moved up to fourth place at the 1972 competition in Spokane.

Miami Central Coach Don Gutzler and his 1974 city championship team

monkey bars for a long time, and when I showed him, he let me stay."

Right from the beginning, Thomas was the hardest worker on the team. When Gutzler pulled into his parking place in the morning, Kurt was standing there waiting for him. They would drink coffee in Gutzler's office and pore over the latest issue of *Modern Gymnast* to get some ideas for practice—which was more of an adventure than you might think. At Miami Central the new gymnastics team never had the gym all to itself. Gutzler not only had to set up his cumbersome equipment with basketballs bouncing all over the place, he frequently had to discipline—shove, arm wrestle, or march to the principal's office—those ruffians who liked to play the knock-the-fag-gymnasts-off-the-high-bar game.

Two months after practice began, Gutzler scheduled a pickup meet with another school. Kurt was leery about trying all six events, preferring to stick with parallel bars and floor exercise. But Gutzler insisted on his being an All-Arounder right from the start. Thomas placed second and Miami Central had won its first gymnastics meet in history. In May of his freshman year, Thomas finished third in the regionals of the Junior Olympics, beaten only by a pair of eighteen-year-olds. The winner automatically qualified for the finals in Colorado Springs, but neither of the eighteen-year-olds felt they could stand up to the competition, so they let Kurt go. He finished dead last.

"It sounds terrible," says Gutzler, "but Kurt needed to get his eyes opened to good gymnastics. Florida was hardly one of the nation's hotbeds. We did win all seven meets in our beginner league, but that wasn't a true test of anything. The Junior Olympics were. When Kurt came back, we set a long-range goal for him to win the Junior Olympics and the short-term goal of working on age-group compulsory exercises, which teach you the basic way to go about mastering each apparatus."

As a sophomore, Thomas was undefeated in high

school competition. He also finished fourth in the 1972 Amateur Athletic Union Junior Olympics, but was outscored by an eighth grader from the Chicago area—Bart Conner. It was their first confrontation. Thomas would win the AAU Juniors the next year (Conner did not compete), but he did become slightly disenchanted with gymnastics at one point. It may have had something to do with the fact that two of his teammates were shot at by a sniper while walking home after practice, or because his mother and sister were about the only people who ever came to see the gymnastics team perform. At any rate, he decided to try wrestling.

"I competed in the ninety-eight-pound class and I even won a few matches," says Kurt. "But when the state champion came in, put me on my back, and humiliated me in front of the whole school, I went right back to gymnastics. I still wasn't all that strong, particularly on rings. Of course, you should have seen me as a hall monitor at school. They had to assign Elvis Peacock, a friend of mine who became a football star at Oklahoma, to patrol the halls with me and act as my enforcer. If I asked a guy for his pass when Peacock wasn't around, it was like I wasn't even there."

Winning the AAU Juniors that year while training under a neophyte coach, in a hostile environment and with some physical shortcomings, helped to create the little ego-monster who emerged as a senior and annihilated everybody in sight—including a visiting men's team from West Germany.

"I was responsible for much of Kurt's cockiness back then," says Gutzler. "I spent a lot of time telling him how great he was because nobody else at Miami Central would. Then, too, he worked so hard he just couldn't imagine anyone beating him. When everybody else was at the beach, he'd be in the gym sweating out a new routine. At night, when they were out cruising, we'd take my key and sneak into our gym or go over to Miami-Dade for a couple more hours of work. Counting phys ed class and our regular two-hour

Though he was no strongman on the rings at this point, Thomas's All-Around performance in Ingelheim, West Germany, helped the United States team qualify for the Olympics.

As a sophomore at Indiana State, Thomas won five medals at the Pan American Games in Mexico City and took fourth place in the 1976 NCAA meet.

practice in the afternoon, he was training five hours a day even back then."

Growing up without a father was not easy for Kurt. Robert Thomas had made a comfortable living for his wife and four children as the manager of a meat company. When he was killed in an auto accident in 1963, the family had to make do with Mrs. Thomas's salary as a secretary. Kurt was only in second grade at the time and the tragedy seemed to have more of an injurious effect on his two older brothers, neither of whom amounted to much in the role-model department. Left to fend for himself most of the time, Kurt's only negative response to all this was to steal a candy bar from the drug store now and then and, later on, to neglect his homework whenever possible in favor of gymnastics. Whereas, the streak of stubborn independence he built up by being on his own so much has served him quite well.

"When I was a senior, my mother and sister moved out of the Miami Central area to a safer part of town," says Kurt. "But I needed to be close to the gym to stay in shape for the high school season and, more importantly, for the 1974 Junior Olympics which were coming up in August after graduation. So myself and a friend rented a house and lived in it by ourselves for six months, doing all the shopping, cooking, and cleaning—and getting jobs on the side to pay for it all."

The only colleges interested in offering Kurt full-ride scholarships were Cornell, Navy, and the Air Force Academy. Unfortunately, his grades weren't good enough to satisfy their entrance requirements. He thought of going to Southern Illinois, or rather Gutzler did, because it was his alma mater and because it had a good reputation in gymnastics. Too good, it seems, because SIU Coach Bill Meade offered Thomas only a partial scholarship and wasn't interested in flying him up to Carbondale for a closer look. Gutzler told Kurt he was worth more than a partial scholarship, so Thomas sat tight and waited for Indiana State to pick up the scent.

Roger Counsil would never have heard about Kurt except for his association with Miami-Dade. Bruce Davis, the junior college coach, had grown up in Indianapolis along with his more famous sister, Muriel Grossfeld. He was one source and Joe Childs, a pommel horse specialist at Miami-Dade, was another. Counsil was in the process of talking Childs into transferring to Indiana State when Childs said to him:

"I also know a good All-Around man you should take a look at."

"How good is he on side horse?"

"He's very good."

A round-trip ticket to Terre Haute was waiting for Thomas at the airport the next day.

"The first time I ever talked to Kurt he said he wanted to be a world champion," says Counsil, "and I think he knew, deep down, that he would be. I felt he had a chance for two reasons. What made the biggest impression on me was his positive attitude and single-mindedness of purpose; I knew that would not only help him, but would be contagious in our gym. Also, he came to Indiana State with no bad habits, nothing we had to change. Just tack on some difficulty and turn him loose!

"As soon as I offered him a full scholarship, he said he would come to Indiana State. He sounded so committed to the idea that I let him fly back to Miami without signing him to a national letter-of-intent. That was an oversight which began to bother me more and more as the summer wore on. I had seen films of Kurt, and I couldn't believe we were getting him so easily. He needed work on his compulsories and wasn't strong by any means on rings. But for a kid coming out of high school *in Florida*, he was a well-balanced All-Arounder. I started thinking that someone was going to sneak in and recruit him away from us. I couldn't reach Kurt by telephone because he was away at Junior Olympics camp. My hands were tied.

"When Kurt finished second, behind Bart Conner, I really began to get worried. But all I could do was

In tribute to his thirty-eight years of coaching at Penn State, the newly retired Wettstone got a free ride at the Olympic trials from Bart Conner, Thomas, Wayne Young and Doug Fitzgerald.

Clowning on the Nittany Lion statue at Penn State after winning the 1976 Olympic trials. From left: meet director and U.S. Team Manager Gene Wettstone, Gene Whelan (alternate), Thomas, Marshall Avener, Tom Beach, Wayne Young, Peter Kormann, Bart Conner, U.S. Coach Karl Schwenzfeier.

wait and hope he'd show up when school began. And the first day of classes, he was here. A kid who kept his word."

The 1974 Junior Olympics was the first one sponsored by the United States Gymnastics Federation. All previous Junior Olympics had been run by the Amateur Athletic Union, and apparently the USGF was having a little trouble getting things coordinated. The meet was held in Algonquin, Illinois, and a crowd of about eighteen people was there to watch. Exact attendance figures don't exist because the meet was held outdoors on a scorching August day. By eleven in the morning the sun's rays had heated the high bar to the point where you couldn't grab hold of it without burning your hands. A makeshift tent had to be erected to shade the apparatus between the routines of the competitors. Compulsories were held in the morning, optionals in the afternoon, and the competition between Kurt and Bart went pretty much the way it is still going today: Bart won the school figures, Kurt won the free-lance stuff; Bart floated through the air like a glider, Kurt cut it like a knife. Only at this point, Bart was still winning the meets.

Thomas finished ninth in the NCAAs as a freshman at Indiana State, but made a much bigger name for himself the next fall when he led a team from the United States to an upset victory over Cuba at the Pan American Games in Mexico City. Thomas finished third in the All-Around, behind two Cubans who were vastly more experienced. He also got his first taste of how nationalism corrupts international meets.

"The Cuban coach was the technical director of the meet," Thomas recalls. "If the United States got a higher score than he wanted, he called a conference and got the score lowered—or at least yelled at the judges. He also changed the order of the competitors in the floor exercise finals, which is never done. In fact, I didn't ever know when I was scheduled to go up on an event. There was never any time to prepare yourself."

Thomas learned some valuable lessons in Mexico City and came home with five medals, including the team gold. But while this was big news in Havana, Terre Haute, and all over Europe, it was virtually ignored in the American press. On Thursday morning, October 23, 1975, most U.S. sports pages were running headlines about day-and-a-half-old news: the classic sixth game of the World Series in which Carlton Fisk's foul-pole homer pulled Boston even with Cincinnati at three games apiece.

However, in U.S. gymnastics circles, Thomas was almost as big a hero as Fisk was in Beantown. After years of promising the world that they were ready to move up to third place in the Olympic standings, the Americans had fallen on their faces at the 1972 Games in Munich. The United States finished tenth out of twelve teams, and its six athletes didn't even average 9.0 per exercise. This was the worst showing ever by an American team—in many ways. One member left the team shortly before the Games, another was injured, and it didn't help matters when two others got into a fist fight. Thomas's Pan Am performances were a signal to the world that at last the United States was developing young gymnasts who could do some damage on the scoreboard. His third-place finish guaranteed him a spot in the 1976 Olympic Trials, and he was one of five new faces who ended up making that team.

Conner was to be another. He clinched that by winning the 1976 American Cup in New York, besting an eighteen-nation field before he had even graduated from high school. Thomas was busy with NCAA action at the time and couldn't compete. But two weeks later at an Olympic qualifying meet in Berkeley, California, Bart beat Kurt again—despite the first 9.9 of Thomas's career (on horse) and his best score ever on high bar, 9.75.

During the next three years, however, Thomas would lose to Conner only once. He started getting even at the 1976 Olympic Trials, where he outdistanced Connor and all other Americans. He was looking so good at training camp, in fact, that *Sports Illustrated* picked him to win a gold medal on the horse in Montreal. Then, during a workout just before the start of the Games, he bent his right index finger backward at a forty-five-degree angle, stretching some ligaments.

Unable to grasp any of the apparatus with authority, Thomas did well to finish twenty-first in the All-Around, beaten by teammates Wayne Young (twelfth) and Peter Kormann (fifteenth) but well ahead of Conner, who didn't qualify for the All-Around. Thomas also narrowly missed the pommel horse finals. While his injured finger was obviously a factor in these failures, in truth, Thomas wasn't ready to beat an Olympic field at anything.

"I was just a kid back then," he says. "I was inexperienced and totally in awe of the whole thing." "The whole thing" referring not only to the quality of the competition, but to the hordes of young female fans who squealed at whatever he did and followed him everywhere.

Coach and athlete sat down after the Olympics and decided it was time to begin establishing a reputation overseas. "Kurt hasn't really learned anything new in gymnastics over the last two years," Counsil announced at the time. "Mostly it's just been polishing and competing. His life has been pretty complicated, what with forty gymnastics meets during that time and him trying to go to school, too. Consequently, he will not compete for Indiana State this year [called "redshirting"] so that he can concentrate on his studies and so we can pick some key international meets for him to compete in."

Thomas's first trip was supposed to take him to the People's Republic of China, but it was postponed twice—once because of earthquakes in China and then because of the death of Mao Tse-tung. When the dates were reset for October 1976, Thomas was incapacitated. He had been opening some beans for dinner one night when the can slipped and toppled off the counter. When something slips out of a gymnast's grasp—

whether it's the high bar or a can of beans—he grabs for it again instinctively. Only Thomas got the razor-sharp lid instead of the can. His right hand was cut from the base of the thumb to the right index finger, and doctors needed fourteen stitches to fix him up. Suddenly Thomas's life was very uncomplicated; instead of competing in Indiana or in China, he was competing nowhere. In short order, he decided this was not the proper time to go looking for an international reputation. He postponed the redshirting idea and turned his attention toward missing as little of the Indiana State season as possible.

Thomas wasn't ready to compete until Christmastime, but by April first he was the NCAA All-Around champion and Indiana State was co-team titlist with Oklahoma. Conner was by this time a freshman at OU, and he closed out the NCAA meet with a 9.55 on parallel bars to forge that incredible team tie, even when carried out to the thousandths place: 434.475 to 434.475. However, Indiana State had Thomas's victory on its side of the ledger and the Sycamores attached great significance to the fact that they won the coin flip and got to take the team trophy back to Terre Haute.

Not only was Thomas the unquestioned champion of the United States, he even managed to sandwich a couple of international meets around his NCAA win. In March 1977, he lost by .1 point to Japan's Mitsuo Tsukahara in the Dial-American Cup in New York. And even Tsukahara, a twenty-nine-year-old, nine-time Olympic medalist, seemed sheepish about the judges' decision. At dinner afterward, he turned to Thomas and attempted to bridge the language barrier with a bit of sign language.

"First he pointed to himself," Kurt recalls. "Then he made a looping motion—up and down—with his hand. Finally he pointed to me and held up his index finger. I knew what he meant: *Tsukahara over the hill, Thomas No. 1.*"

Then three weeks after the NCAAs, Thomas and

Indiana State and Oklahoma shared the NCAA team championship in 1977, but Thomas ran away with the All-Around.

Kurt and his wife Beth

Counsil were in Cluj Napoca, Romania, being introduced to international judging, Eastern European-style. The occasion was the 1977 Romanian Invitational and the curious hometown judging and scorekeeping which took place there caused an angry Counsil to remark, "This is a *sport*?" Thomas was hot as a pistol and won the meet anyway, prompting one of his most oft-used quotes when on foreign soil over the next few years: "They may try to screw you, but if you go through your routines without any breaks, they can't."

Over the summer, Thomas won the second of his three straight USGF national titles, and by fall 1977—with one year of college eligibility still remaining—he was ready for his redshirt season. What's more, he had already acquired a significant following overseas. When he first unveiled the Thomas Flair at the 1975 Criterium Cup in Barcelona, the crowd went crazy ("The loudest gasp I've ever heard," says Counsil). Spanish newspaper headlines proclaimed Thomas's style "the New Gymnastics," and the stories said that here at last was an innovator from America who wasn't following in the footsteps of either the Japanese or the Russians.

Gymnasts seem to need as much encouragement and psychological reinforcement as any athletes alive, and during the heydays of 1977, Thomas was getting his from three different sources.

Following the Olympics, he underwent a spiritual transformation and began pursuing a Christian way of life. This seemed to buoy his confidence. "I believe in myself more since this has happened to me," he said. "But I'm not just doing it for myself. I'm doing it through Jesus Christ and I feel a whole lot better about everything." There was also the PMA craze that swept through the ISU gym, spearheaded by one of Kurt's teammates, Barry Woodward. "PMA" stands for *Positive Mental Attitude*, from the inspirational text written by W. Clement Stone. For a while that's all you heard about around the gym. To Kurt, things were either "good for my PMA" or "bad for my PMA," and

anybody who was responsible for the latter was ordered out of the gym. Throw in a team Bible study group which met once a week and the theme from *Rocky* which played over and over again during workouts, and you had an ultrapositive environment for gymnastics.

As the year went on, however, Kurt talked more and more about Beth Osting, the Indiana State student he was "almost engaged to," and less and less about the Bible and PMA.

"I met him at a sorority party," says Beth. "I thought he was some high school kid they were showing around. He started following me and I told him to get lost. Then my girlfriends told me who he was, and that he was a creep with a cocky reputation. I'm just a farm girl from Rushville, Indiana, so I wasn't impressed that he was a gymnast. I went out with him more as a challenge. I figured I'd show him! But then when I got to know him, he was nice. I liked him."

By summer, Kurt and Beth had decided to get married, but when they sat down to plan a fall wedding, this is what Kurt's travel itinerary looked like:

Oct. 6–9	USGF Congress—Memphis, Tennessee
Oct. 9–13	Criterium Cup—Barcelona, Spain
Oct. 14–23	Training camp in Montceau-les-Mines, France
Oct. 23–31	Competition in Oviedo, Spain
Nov. 1	Arrive in Terre Haute
Nov. 9–22	Chunichi Cup—Tokyo, Japan
Nov. 23	Arrive in USA
Nov. 24–27	Four-nation meet—Münster, West Germany
Nov. 28	Great Britain Invitational
Dec. 9	Return to Terre Haute

Unfortunately for Beth, her folks, the minister, and the caterers, this turned out to be a mere facsimile of Kurt's actual travel and competitive plans. All told, the wedding date was changed six different times

In order to win medals at the Olympics or World Championships, a gymnast must establish a reputation with important international judges. That means competing in Europe.

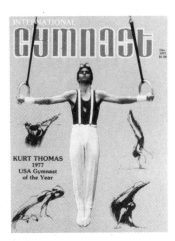

before the couple settled on December 31, 1977. Beth knew there wouldn't be a meet on New Year's Eve.

"I'll bet ten coaches talked to Kurt during the time we were engaged and told him not to get married," says Beth. "Some of them got really pushy, too. They told him that having a wife around would hurt his gymnastics, or they turned it around and said he would probably have a rotten marriage, maybe even end up divorced because of all the time he'd have to spend training, traveling, and competing. The thing is, I never begrudged Kurt any of that time. In fact, I work out with him sometimes. But I think even Coach Counsil was worried about our getting married until he got to know me. It was a difficult time for us. I felt a lot of people were against me."

Counsil must have become reconciled to the rightness of the decision, because he spent New Year's Eve as his prize pupil's best man. And Thomas silenced the rest of the skeptics when he took his new bride to New York in March and won all six events at the 1978 Dial-American Cup. East German Olympian Roland Bruckner finished second, Conner was third, Russia's Sergei Khizniakov was fourth, and Tsukahara —who had predicted as much the year before—was fifth. In the interview room afterward, Thomas told the New York press how he and his wife couldn't afford a real honeymoon trip when they got married and that this was his wedding present to her.

Beth, on the other hand, was worried that every trip she made with her husband from now on was going to be like this one. At the awards ceremony after the meet, hundreds of young girls spilled out onto the Madison Square Garden floor shrieking and crying for Kurt's autograph as though he were a Beatle or something. In the crush, one of them even mistook Beth for a fellow groupie.

"Do you think Kurt will sign my book?"

"Well, I don't know. He's awfully tired and would probably like to get going."

"How do you know so much? Hey, didn't I see him talking to you during the meet? Who do you think you are, his mother or something?"

"No, I'm his wife."

"Oh, no . . ."

From that point on, Beth began to take a much greater interest in reading and answering Kurt's fan mail for him. One letter, postmarked three days after the American Cup was seen on ABC-TV, was addressed to "Kurt c/o Indiana State University." That was it, but the letter got to him. Another, from a fan in England, was addressed to "Mr. Kurt Thomas, Indiana State University, *Florida*, U.S.A." It also reached him.

The most pathetic groupie letter Thomas ever received was hand-delivered to him in Florida by a fifteen-year-old girl from Pennsylvania who appeared on his doorstep one night saying she had run away from home to live with him. The incident occurred shortly after the 1976 Olympics, as Thomas was vacationing and visiting old friends in Miami.

"It was a rainy night or I never would have let her in the door to begin with," Thomas recalls. "I was sure she must be pregnant and that she wanted me to take the rap. I told her I was going to call her mother, but she flipped out and started showing me these sick love letters she had written to herself—and signed my name to. That's when I began to remember her face. She had asked me to pose for a picture at the Olympic Trials at Penn State, and then I thought I had seen her with a camera in her hand when I was at the U.S. training camp in Montreal. I even remembered getting a call from someone who said she had sneaked out of the house so she could call me from a pay phone. I asked this girl if that was her, and she said it was. How she tracked me down, I have no idea. But I knew I had to call her mother. This time she gave me the number, but her mother said to hell with her—she didn't have enough money to get her home from Florida. I didn't want to tell this girl to go fly a kite. So like a real sucker, I gave her thirty bucks for a ticket,

A full-twist catch, where Thomas must let go of the bar, turn completely around in mid-air and catch hold of it again.

plus some meal money, and put her on a bus to Pittsburgh."

When a person elicits this kind of adoration from perfect strangers, that's what is known as "star quality." And when Kurt arrived in Los Angeles in July 1978 for the annual USGF meet, the Hollywood agents were waiting for him.

"Kurt, I've seen what you can do in gymnastics and, believe me, you have all the tools to become great," said Paul Brandon, who also handles Bill Bixby. "I'm calling you now because I screwed up in not getting to Bruce Jenner early. I don't want to make the same mistake twice."

Art Smith, of the Agency for Media Artists in Beverly Hills, scoffed at that line. "Listen, there are a lot of sharks in this business," he said as Thomas was coming off the mat after winning his third straight USGF title. "Don't sign with anybody until you talk to me."

Kurt had just answered a 9.85 score from Conner with a 9.9 on high bar, and he was clearly enjoying Smith's earnestness. "Well, some guy called me today and offered me a movie part," said Kurt. "I'm supposed to play a body builder when he was a little kid. What do you think about that?"

"Hey," said Smith, "you don't have to settle for small potatoes."

It's a big jump from reading gymnastics magazines with Gutzler to figure out what you're going to do at practice, to speculating about your future in show biz with Hollywood agents. But it's like Kurt says about learning the triple flyaway: You do it in stages. If all you're looking for is a little fun, then winning the Miami city championship is enough. If you want to be remembered as a serious gymnast, then taking five medals at the Pan American Games is plenty. If you just want to say you took part in the Olympics, then twenty-first place is fine. And if your primary interest is to become a star, then winning six events in Madison Square Garden will do the trick. But if you know, deep down, that you have the talent to become a world champion, you have to keep going.

It all depends on your expectations, and as he packed his bags for Strasbourg, France, Kurt Thomas's were extremely high.

1978 World Championships, Strasbourg, France

Diary of a Gold Medal

Tuesday, Oct. 10
Terre Haute/Chicago

Leaving Indiana to compete in Europe is like travel-ing to another planet. That thought hit me today as I kissed Beth good-bye in the doorway of our house trailer and headed down the driveway toward Stras-bourg, France, and the World Gymnastics Champion-ships. In Terre Haute, I'm nothing special because—as is the case in most parts of the country—gymnastics is nothing special here. People know me on the street because my picture is in the papers from time to time and because I did something-or-other in the 1976 Olympics, which doesn't happen to an Indiana State student very often.

But this campus revolves around Larry Bird, the All-American basketball player. You see his name in neon above liquor stores ("The Indiana State Bird Is Larry") and ten times as many people show up to see him perform as to see me. I guess that figures, what with the following basketball has in the state of Indiana. But sometimes I feel like grabbing people on the street and dragging them into a gymnastics meet so they can see what they're missing by not coming to see our team perform.

There were exactly five people at the Terre Haute airport to see us off today as Coach Counsil and I boarded a little Allegheny commuter plane for a fifty-five-minute flight to Chicago. Which is five people more than I expected. It seems like you have to leave town to get any recognition. When I've appeared on talk shows, I've been flown to Los Angeles, picked up at the airport by a chauffeur-driven limousine, and had my name printed on my dressing room door when I arrived at the studio. On the other hand, I have a community-health professor at Indiana State who hates me. I walked into class one day after I had just gotten back from winning a big meet overseas, and he said to me, "I'm jealous as hell of your accomplishments and I'm never cutting you any slack in this course!" Hey, I don't expect free As, but that's really great, isn't it?

I've spent five years in this town with its God-awful winters and its 130 railroad crossings, I don't even have enough money to put gas in my van, and here's a guy who thinks I'm a prima donna.

Met the rest of the U.S. team at O'Hare and made our connection to a SwissAir flight that took off at 6:45 P.M. We land in Zurich tomorrow morning at 10 A.M. My mood is no better, but I decided to stay awake long enough for dinner.

The problem with being a gymnast in the United States is the same as being a discus thrower, a high jumper or any other kind of amateur athlete—you can't make a living at it. You could, but you're not allowed to. Which is why I already feel like a man out of work even though I'm still in college. Maybe someday I won't. Gordon Maddux, the ABC commentator, just told me that gymnastics has moved up to second place behind auto racing in the Nielsen ratings that ABC uses to plan its programming schedule. I guess that's why ABC is televising the World Championships and anything else it can get its hands on in gymnastics.

It's a different story being a world-class gymnast in a country like the Soviet Union. Take Nikolai Andri-anov, the Russian All-Arounder who has been the best gymnast in the world since 1975. He isn't No. 1 in his country either. But I saw a wire service story the other day that said he had finished third in the voting for USSR Athlete of the Year behind a chess player and a high jumper. I'd be 207th in the voting over here, behind Affirmed—and his stable boy.

Larry Bird and I are pretty friendly, and we respect each other's talents. But neither one of us has the time to see the other one perform. If I happen to run into Larry in the gym, I'll say, "How ya doin', Larry?" He'll say, "Okay, Kurt. How're you?" There we are: the two greatest athletes in Indiana State's history. Only Larry Bird is a cinch millionaire when he leaves school, and I'm about to lose my 10 percent discount at the Bonanza Steak House.

The stewardess just came by with the headphones.

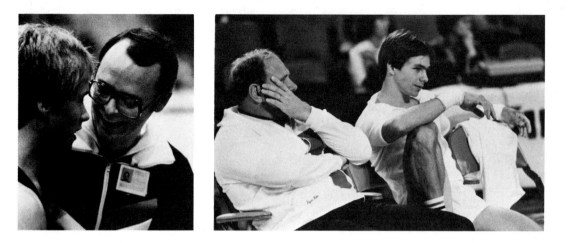

I said no thanks. It's a nine-hour flight to Zurich and I just took a couple Dalmanes. I've seen the Atlantic before.

Wednesday, Oct. 11
Zurich/Lucerne

When I walked off the plane in Switzerland, I felt about 200 percent better, like I was suddenly on important international business. Slept about three-quarters of the way, and Mike Wilson, my roommate on this trip, didn't wake up until they flashed the seat-belt sign as we were coming in for a landing.

We are taking a bus ride to Lucerne through some incredibly beautiful mountains, and I feel like I'm part of an elite group. The World Championships are the biggest event in gymnastics—except for the Olympics, of course—and our team has a good chance to finish third behind the Japanese and the Russians and win a bronze medal. No one expects us to do it but ourselves. My personal goal, a tough but realistic one, is to finish in the top six in the All-Around and win a medal someplace. I'm not counting on winning a gold. Not because America hasn't won one in international competition since 1932, but because I don't need to put that kind of pressure on myself right now. I can't beat Andrianov; the time isn't right in the judges' minds, and I'm probably not good enough yet. But I'm coming hard. Jet lag or no jet lag, this is definitely better. Our bags even made it.

Thursday, Oct. 12
Lucerne

The World Championships don't get underway until October 23, but our team came over to Europe early in order to get in a warmup meet with Norway, Great Britain, and Switzerland. I'm glad. Lucerne is a beautiful spot and I know I can relax here. My battle plan for tomorrow night's competition is to go hard physically and take it easy mentally. I want to win the meet, but I don't want to show anything too difficult. I'll save

my 1½ twisting, 1¾ somersault on floor exercise for Strasbourg.

We are surrounded by mountains here, one of which we climbed today—by cable car and by gondola, that is. It is called the Stanserhorn, it is 6,300 feet high, and from the top we could look down and see the clouds. There isn't one like it in Terre Haute. Did a little shopping, too, although every other shop in Lucerne is a jeweler's. What else?

Our team, as a whole, is pulling together and looking good in workouts, although Bart Conner and I haven't been seen at the same apparatus yet. I doubt that's much of an accident. Bart is really intent upon beating me these days, and I know he has told people that he feels his chances are better if the two of us aren't so friendly—which we normally are. I like Bart. But I remember not liking it much when he used to beat me all the time in the Juniors, so I know what he's going through.

I haven't cared for Bart's coach at the University of Oklahoma, Paul Ziert, ever since he referred to the rest of the nation's gymnasts as "plumbers" after Oklahoma won the 1978 NCAA title. Ziert does know his gymnastics, however, and he is the assistant coach on this tour. I realize there isn't one single, perfect method of coaching, but I'm thankful that my coach at Indiana State, Roger Counsil, who is the head coach of the U.S. team, handles me differently than Ziert handles Bart. Counsil gives me some freedom to be myself. I was a wise-ass little punk from Miami when he first saw me, but he had the courage to give me a lot of rope—enough to hang myself probably—in hopes that I'd really find myself as a gymnast and as a person. I was impossible to deal with as a freshman—a fast-talking, know-it-all street kid with a little bit of talent to back it up. I had a lot of growing up to do. Whereas Bart, coming from a nice middle-class family in suburban Chicago, probably didn't. Nevertheless, Ziert smothers Bart. Or mothers him, you might say. I've seen Ziert reach over and slap Bart's hands when he caught Bart chewing on a hangnail. Ziert is a genius at gymnastics, but I'm not sure he's right for Bart. As a high school senior, Bart won the American Cup at Madison Square Garden. He was out of sight. I was a sophomore at Indiana State at the time and I couldn't touch him. But in the last couple years, I've beaten Bart nine out of ten times. I know, because I've kept track. I'm sure Bart has, too. He's super smooth and a good technician, but he plays it too safe. What he needs is less attention spent on compulsories and greater difficulty in his optionals. In other words, he needs to stop being a plumber. I wonder if Ziert ever tells *him* that!

What's ironic about me rooming with Mike Wilson is that he is a teammate of Bart's at Oklahoma and another pupil of Ziert's. Except that Mike doesn't get the same treatment from Ziert that Bart does. Ziert thinks Mike would be a lot better gymnast if he devoted less time to the Fellowship of Christian Athletes and worked harder at gymnastics. Mike is really a good gymnast, I think, and we've been helping each other a lot over here. Mostly little things, like making sure the parallel bars are the right distance apart before the other guy goes up. But it's important to go around in workouts with someone you're comfortable with, and Mike and I seem to enjoy each other's company. We have something else in common: We each miss our women. Mike is getting married soon to a girl he met at Oklahoma. Beth is coming over on the same flight with the U.S. women's team and is due in Monday morning.

Friday, Oct. 13
Lucerne/Stans

I always have something wrong with me on the day of a meet. If I don't have, I'll find something or make something up. Maybe that's one of my superstitions. Today, my shoulders and hamstrings are sore. We took a bus to the four-nation meet and on the way Coach Counsil announced the order in which we would com-

pete within our team on each event during compulsories. I was last every time—the best position to score high. Bart was next-to-last. That psyched me up, although I wondered if my teammates thought I was our strongest competitor in every event.

The atmosphere at the arena in Stans, Switzerland, was more like an Oktoberfest than a gymnastics meet. We walked in the door and immediately found ourselves in the midst of an indoor fair. There must have been a hundred picnic tables set up around the floor with maybe five hundred chairs. Most of them were filled with people eating sausages and drinking wine or beer. And from what I could tell, they continued eating sausages and drinking wine or beer all night long, cheering just as loudly for those who won tenspeed bikes at a raffle as for us gymnasts out on the floor.

Our first event as a team was the horse, and everybody really hit. This particular Swiss horse was the fattest I had ever seen—in keeping with many of the spectators. It had unbelievably soft ends, which made maneuvering from one side to the other extremely difficult. Still, I pulled out a 9.45 for the highest score of the night on the horse. By the end of the compulsories, we were so far ahead I wondered how much good the meet was going to do us. Mike and I talked about the Book of Revelations until 12:30, then turned out the light.

Saturday, Oct. 14
Lucerne/Stans

We got dressed in our red, white, and blue U.S. warmups and went up on top of another mountain to meet the mayor of Lucerne for lunch. The guys were all hoping it would turn out to be Mount Titlis, a piece of scenery we had discovered in our guidebooks. But it wasn't.

The meet tonight was great. I had a lot of strength and endurance in my optionals and scored three 9.75s —on horse, parallel bars, and high bars. Our team won

Strasbourg, France
Eizo Kenmotsu of Japan, who has won twenty-three Olympic and World Championship medals in his career

by 12.5 points, which is a lot. I won, too, beating Bart by 3.05, which is also a lot. However, for the first time, he really showed me what a tough, gritty competitor he can be. And friendshipwise, we seem back to normal. I'm psyched to the max!

Monday, Oct. 16
Lucerne / Strasbourg

I don't know where Beth is. The women's team flight was delayed, so, naturally, our bus is leaving for Strasbourg without them.

Reminds me of the time I flew by myself from Tokyo to Alaska to Düsseldorf to join a U.S. team headed for a meet in West Germany. Only the team got to Düsseldorf an hour early and left without me. I was totally burned out, I'd blown most of my money in Japan buying thirty-dollar silk shirts for the groomsmen in my wedding, and what's more, I didn't even know the name of the competition I was headed for. I called the U.S. consulate in Düsseldorf and explained my problem. "Where is the meet?" they asked. "In Münster," I said. "Which one?" they replied. That's when I knew I was in trouble. I called Counsil in the States and told him I wanted to come home. He talked me out of it by reminding me that I needed to establish a reputation with international judges. He was right, except I was closer to establishing a reputation for vagrancy by this time. I had twenty dollars in my pocket and I was starving. Fortunately, a kindly West German helped me buy a train ticket to the right Münster—I was calling it "Monster" by this time—and rode with me most of the way. From the airport, we took a subway and at least four different trains. The last one made twenty stops, and by the time I got to Münster, I was sitting in between two cars huddled up against the cold. There were no seats inside the train and not even enough room to stand. I was also muttering to myself about how rotten being a gymnast was. It's funny though, I've thought a lot about that trip over the years and I think it helped me a great deal—as a

person as well as a gymnast. I ended up finishing second to Eberhard Gienger in that meet, which was great for me although I thought I should have won, and it made a mark for me in Europe. In a way, I owe it all to some good Samaritan from West Germany—I didn't even get his name—who helped me run up and down the right stairs.

Just got off the bus in Strasbourg, the "Crossroads of Europe," after a four-hour bus ride. I heard somebody raving about the scenery, but I slept all the way.

Tuesday, Oct. 17
Strasbourg

Beth arrived and all seems well, although the warm atmosphere between competing nations that I remember from the Olympics is missing here. For one thing, there is no Olympic-village setup as there was in Montreal. The thirty-three nations represented at these World Championships are spread out in different hotels and it's hard to socialize and get your training in, too. I love the Japanese guys, especially Mitsuo Tsukahara and Eizo Kenmotsu; even though they speak only a few words of English, we can communicate and have a good time. They are staying right here at our hotel, but they are deadly serious this week. I can tell, because Japanese gymnasts are notorious for drinking and smoking until all hours. Here, they are only smoking. That's another thing about the prevailing mood here. Everybody knows that Moscow in 1980 is going to be a bear, and they're starting to get ready for it already. The Russians will be sky high and the Japanese will be hard-pressed to keep the Olympic team title they've won five times in a row—since 1960. Consequently, they are doing everything as a group here. When Tsukahara goes out to do some stretching exercises on the sidewalk in forty-five-degree weather, they all go. I've been watching Kenmotsu in practice and I think he is going to throw a giant swing on parallel bars. That's never been done before, so I know the Japanese are pulling out all stops.

Opening ceremonies, Hall
Rhenus

The American men. Left to right:
Jim Hartung, Bart Conner, Tim
LaFleur (alternate), Peter Kormann,
Thomas, Mike Wilson.

Bart Conner, fully extended on a compulsory straddle toe-touch

Sunday, Oct. 22
Strasbourg

My strategy in Switzerland was to stay relaxed mentally and go hard physically, but I can tell the World Championships are only a day away. After a week of training, I'm starting to get nervous. I'm lying in bed trying to remember how I felt before the Olympics. I really can't remember, except I know it couldn't have been this bad. I had a sprained finger in Montreal—hooray, a real injury for once!—and I was probably busy worrying about that. All I'm telling myself here is: Get through the team compulsories without a major break.

Monday, Oct. 23
Strasbourg

I made it! No major breaks. Even got a 9.75 on high bar. Compulsories aren't my best suit, mainly because I can't show off any of my tricks. You have to be content with doing a series of prescribed moves as well as you can. Still, I'm happy to be in ninth place with a score of 57.4. Bart is dogging my tracks in tenth with 57.35 and the team is doing super! Right now we're fourth, trailing the East Germans 285 to 283.1. Bronze medal, here we come!

Tuesday, Oct. 24
Strasbourg

There will be four days of competition here: team compulsories and team optionals, individual All-Around and individual apparatus. But with a day off in between for the women's competition, it takes an entire week to complete this meet. The days off are good for your body, but bad for your nerves. You think too much. I've been keeping this diary for three years—ever since the 1975 Pan Am Games, when I won five medals and convinced myself that I could compete internationally. But it is getting increasingly harder for me to write anything down. I'm so hyper. Not to the point of being mentally drained. It's the opposite. I'm adren-

alized! Ready to go! Psyched to the max!

Wednesday, Oct. 25
Strasbourg

Optionals night. I started out on horse, just as I had in Switzerland. I thought that would bring me good luck. It didn't. I can't believe that after all the time I've spent doing my Flair, I broke slightly in the middle of it. I think I was just so horse crazy—everybody kept saying I was going to win a medal on it—that I ended up putting a lot of pressure on myself after all. I scored 9.65, and things didn't go much better after that. Bart and I did the best routines of our lives on parallel bars and got screwed. I even stuck a double pike dismount and the judges gave me a 9.50! Counsil protested my score, but an East German or Russian judge, I forget which, ruled that he hadn't registered his complaint within the required amount of time. Right. Although you expect it in Europe, this was the first real sign of anti-American prejudice in judging we had seen since we left home. I think the team was kind of down when we got back to our hotel. It was around nine P.M. when Bart and Paul Ziert figured up the scores, but regardless of how the math turned out, I knew we had missed our chance at the bronze team medal. However, our score, 568.7, was something to be proud of. It gave us fourth place, behind Japan—they did it again!—the USSR, and East Germany. And it was more than twelve points higher than our team score in Montreal, when we finished a distant seventh—beaten by Hungary, West Germany, and Romania, as well as the others. We have improved the equivalent of 9.3 to 9.5 per man, and we all knew how much better we could have done than that.

After practically falling off the high bar tonight, I figured myself for about twentieth place in the standings for tomorrow night's All-Around finals. When I heard I was twelfth, I was surprised. Bart is eleventh, leading me by .05 of a point. Got to beat him! I can still make the top six!

Thursday, Oct. 26
The Black Forest

To see this part of Germany—on our schedule—you have to get up pretty early in the morning. We crawled out of bed and onto a Mercedes Benz bus at 6:30 A.M. Stopped at some quaint little sixteenth-century villages that looked like they were right out of a postcard—cobblestone streets, pastry shops, and all. I bought some expensive coffee, Beth got a cream puff. She was excited, but I thought the Black Forest looked like just another bunch of trees. I slept most of the trip. That's why I needed the coffee.

Friday, Oct. 27
Strasbourg

Becoming the best All-Around gymnast in the world means as much to me as winning the decathlon did to Bruce Jenner, and this afternoon I went a little crazy thinking about it. I started bobbing and weaving around the hotel room like Muhammad Ali, really hyper-psyched to move up in the standings. Beth tried to calm me down, but I was in some kind of zone. I turned toward the door, made a loud grunt like some black belt in karate, and—*Wham!*—I butted my head into the door and made a huge hole. At least, it seemed huge to Beth. Guys on my team at Indiana State are always head-butting things, but I never had until now. I was so pumped up, it didn't even hurt. Beth was the one who was crying. This is a really nice hotel and she is convinced we'll have to pay for a whole new door. She just said we'll probably have to spend the rest of the week out on the street.

I feel a little guilty, but all I can think about is moving up, moving up. I told Bart before the meet that we could still make our goals. I knew he could make the top ten, but inside I didn't think I could make it up to sixth. It may sound terrible, but I still wanted to beat Bart at all costs.

After four events, I finally saw my name, "Thomas, USA," come up on the leader board—I was in sixth place and really cooking! I'd already done a piked Tsukahara with a full twist on the vault and gotten a 9.8! That was only my highest vault score ever, and I'd saved it for the World Championships! I forgot about the big names that I was up against and kicked it real hard right until the end, finishing with another 9.8 on floor.

Top six—I made it! I knew it before the numbers even hit the scoreboard. I had beaten four of the six Russians and four Japanese. I reminded myself that sixth was all I had come for, except that if I hadn't botched up my Flair on the horse and hadn't made a few other minor breaks here and there, I might have come close to winning a medal.

I didn't think Bart and the other guys on the team seemed that happy for me. Bart got ninth himself, which was great, seeing how most experts didn't rank any Americans in the top twenty in the world a year ago. But he only shook my hand once. On the other hand, how would I have acted if he had beaten me? I watched Andrianov and Alexander Ditiatin, the Russians who finished one-three in the All-Around. They only shook hands once.

I went off to dinner with Beth and tried not to feel pissed that I hadn't given Andrianov a run for his money. I had a steak burned to the max.

Saturday, Oct. 28
Strasbourg

Another day off before the last day of competition—the finals on each of the six individual apparatus. I am a finalist in floor exercise and an alternate on horse, parallel bars, and high bar. All in all, things have gone well here, but something is missing, something I can't put my finger on. Maybe it's that our team is still so far behind the Russians. They are *impressive*. Ditiatin is a real stud and he sticks his dismounts every time. Andrianov may have bad form, but he is still the best and most exciting gymnast in the world. He's so strong, and with those foam-covered pits they have to land in

Bus ride to the Black Forest

This was the last international meet that Nikolai Andrianov was to dominate.

Thomas's floor exercise routine received a 9.9 from the judges, which made him the first American in forty-six years to win a gold medal in international gymnastics competition.

over in the Soviet Union, he's never afraid of height in his floor exercise. He is the only gymnast in the world who does a double layout somersault, meaning he keeps his entire body straight—not tucked or piked—throughout two midair revolutions. I'm wondering when we'll be able to chop him down to size.

Sunday, Oct. 29
Strasbourg

I woke up feeling woozy. A cold, I guess, or more of my day-of-the-meet superstitions. Except I looked so bad during warmups, Beth came over and told me I shouldn't compete.

Andrianov came into the floor-ex finals with a .1 lead over me and Roland Bruckner of East Germany, as a result of our scores on floor during the team competition. He's already won more than a dozen gold medals in international competition and all he needed to do, given his clout with the judges, was to make four strong passes across the mat.

I was looking right at Andrianov when he missed his famous double layout somersault and landed on his knees. That cost him .3 of a point, and right then and there I knew Kurt Thomas of the United States was going to win his first gold medal.

I needed a difficult mount, and I really nailed the 1½ twisting, 1¾ somersault. Most of the people in the crowd thought I had landed on my head until they saw me roll out of it and spin around for my second pass. From that point on, it was all automatic. I stuck my dismount, put both fists in the air—which Coach Counsil told me never to do—and strutted off like I was hot stuff. Counsil doesn't go for hot-dogging in international competition, and I tend to agree with him. But when he congratulated me on the sidelines, he was doing his share of hot-dogging, too.

A gold medal!

After you win one, you have to go pick it up. So while I was sitting around waiting to hear my name called and chewing on a Goomie Bear, which is the European version of Jujyfruits, I started remembering the parade of U.S. gold-medal winners I had seen at the Montreal Olympics. I thought about all those swimmers and track guys up there on the victory platform with "The Star-Spangled Banner" playing—which we never, ever hear in our sport—and I realized that was what I had been missing this week. But not anymore. They were just about ready to call my name, and Counsil was really losing his cool. "Kurt, this is one of those special moments in life," he said. "Go out there and ham it up."

I was in your basic trance. I did manage to raise my arms in the air before bending forward to have the gold medal placed around my neck. And then I did something I never do: I started singing the national anthem. I *never* sing the national anthem, anytime or anywhere. And this wasn't a case of me saying to myself, "Now Kurt, be proud you're an American." I just started singing and staring at the flag, without even thinking about it. Anybody who saw me bow my head and close my eyes right at the end probably thought I was praying. I guess I was. But I was also saying to myself, "This is soooooo great, there's just gotta be more of it!"

Monday, Oct. 30
Strasbourg

When we checked out of the hotel today, we took Beth's long black dress off the back of the door where she had it hanging all week to cover up the hole I'd butted in the door. We replaced the dress with a Hotel Novotel decal that fit neatly over the hole. Now nobody will ever remember I was in France.

On second thought, yeah they will.

Congratulations from
Czechoslovakia's Jiri Tabak

Kurt Thomas, triumphant as the
first American to win a gold medal
in international competition in almost half a century

19th WORLD CHAMPIONSHIP
OCTOBER 22-29, 1978
STRASBOURG

ALL AROUND • MEN

		FX	PH	R	V	PB	HB	PRELIM	TOTAL
1.	Andrianov, Nikolai (USSR) ...	9.85	9.70	9.90	9.85	9.75	9.85	58.300	117.200
2.	Kenmotsu, Eizo (JAP)	9.60	9.75	9.80	9.80	9.80	9.75	58.050	116.550
3.	Ditiatin, Alexander (USSR) ...	9.60	9.75	9.70	9.80	9.75	9.80	57.975	116.375
4.	Gienger, Eberhard (FRG).....	9.65	9.75	9.65	9.80	9.70	9.80	57.850	116.200
5.	Kajiyama, Hiroji (JAP)	9.55	9.70	9.60	9.80	9.70	9.60	57.950	115.900
6.	Thomas, Kurt (USA)........	9.80	9.75	9.50	9.80	9.65	9.75	57.475	115.725
7.	Kasamatsu, Shigeru (JAP).....	9.75	8.90	9.70	9.70	9.75	9.80	58.025	115.625
8.	Delchev, Stoyan (BUL).......	9.75	9.55	9.40	9.60	9.75	9.50	57.675	115.225
9.	Conner, Bart (USA).........	9.60	9.80	9.55	9.70	9.65	9.40	57.500	115.200
10.	Nikolay, Michael (GDR)	9.40	9.80	9.30	9.80	9.70	9.75·	57.425	115.175
11.	Tkachev, Alexander (USSR)...	9.75	8.70	9.70	9.80	9.75	9.55	57.825	115.075
12.	Magyar, Zoltan (HUN).......	9.55	9.85	9.30	9.75	9.70	9.65	57.250	115.050
13.	Bruckner, Roland (GDR)	9.60	9.70	9.50	9.75	9.50	9.70	57.025	114.775
14.	Barthel, Ralph (GDR)........	9.60	9.50	9.55	9.70	9.55	9.65	56.900	114.450
15.	Kovacs, Peter (HUN).........	9.65	9.50	9.55	9.75	9.40	9.70	56.650	114.200
16.	Donath, Ferenc (HUN)	9.50	9.65	9.65	9.20	8.95	9.60	57.400	113.950
17.	Rohrwick, Volker (FRG)......	9.40	9.50	9.50	9.65	9.60	9.60	56.675	113.925
17.	Moy, Willie (FRA)	9.70	9.70	9.60	9.75	9.20	9.55	56.425	113.925
19.	Bretscher, Robert (SWI)	9.60	9.60	9.50	9.85	9.50	9.55	56.250·	113.850
20.	Wilson, Mike (USA).........	9.80	9.70	9.40	9.75	9.45	9.30	56.400	113.800

INDIVIDUAL APPARATUS • MEN

FLOOR EXERCISES

		C/O avg.	Final	Total
1.	Thomas, Kurt (USA)	9.750	9.900	19.650
2.	Kasamatsu, Shigeru (JAP)	9.725	9.850	19.575
3.	Ditiatin, Alexander (USSR)..............................	9.700	9.700	19.400
4.	Andrianov, Nikolai (USSR).............................	9.850	9.500	19.350
5.	Deltchev, Stoyan (BUL)	9.700	9.500	19.200
6.	Jorek, Edgar (FRG)	9.725	9.450	19.175
7.	Bruckner, Roland (GDR)...............................	9.750	9.100	18.850
8.	Tabak, Jiri (CSSR)...................................	9.725	8.900	18.625

FX-Floor Exercise / PH-Pommel Horse / R-Rings / V-Vault / PB-Parallel Bars / HB-High Bar

Part Two

How to Watch a Meet

It is widely assumed that the trick to enjoying a men's gymnastics meet is to merely sit back in one's seat and enjoy the tricks. Double twisting somersaults, Maltese crosses, little men swinging madly around a high bar with the aplomb of wind-up toys—it's such a dazzling visual show of technique, strength, and nerve that most people in the stands, even those who come often, tend to overlook the serious head-to-head competition going on between the gymnasts. Granted, there is something entrancing about watching perhaps the most beautiful, the most intricate, and the most difficult-to-achieve physical disciplines in the world of sport. And for those who are seeing their first live meet, having watched gymnastics only on television, ooh-ing and ah-ing tends to dominate all other concerns.

But what really discourages spectators from getting involved in the competitive aspect of men's gymnastics the way they would in, say, a golf tournament is that they find the format, the judging, the terminology, and the mathematics of the scorekeeping beyond their powers of comprehension; as complex, in their eyes, as the routines they see out on the floor.

The scene itself is intimidating enough and does little to dissuade a spectator from these feelings of inadequacy, particularly if this is the first live meet he has ever seen. After all, when as many as six events are going on at one time—as is sometimes the case in the NCAA championships, the World Championships, and the Olympics—one can come away feeling that he missed more gymnastics than he actually saw. Another problem is that most people don't really know how a gymnast wins and loses points, and they aren't convinced the judges do either. When they see a move they like, they have no idea what to call it. And long after they've learned to recognize a 9.8 routine, they still can't figure out what the totals on the scoreboard mean. In other words, they are unable to make the transition from spectator to fan.

At first they don't care. To reduce this beautiful and artistic display of acrobatics to a bunch of decimal points seems ludicrous—like saying that Mikhail Baryshnikov leads Gelsey Kirkland 19.55 to 18.65 after two acts of *Swan Lake*. Except that a person can sustain these feelings of wide-eyed wonder for only so long; after an hour and a half of watching double twisting somersaults, one's appetite for double twisting somersaults is dulled somewhat. The mind yearns for a reference point. What do you have to do to score a 10.0? Why isn't my favorite leading the meet? Whose double twister was the best? What does it all mean?

To figure it out, you must learn to keep score. The electronic scoreboard is no good to you because invariably it's at least one event behind. Besides, keeping tabs on the leaders will get you involved in other aspects of the meet. For example, you don't want to be caught ooh-ing and ah-ing over a good-looking 9.6 routine when your notepad or calculator could have told you that the gymnast needed loads more difficulty in his exercise if he expected to score high enough to move up in the standings. Look at it this way: Horse players don't fret over the complexities of odds, times-in-the-money, and jockeys' records. Everybody at the track carries a program in one hand and a Racing Form in the other. Especially the first-timers. They start out by doing a little reading, then they ask some questions, finally someone tells them they can go to the paddock and get a closer look at the horses before the race. Before long, the guy who didn't know a thing about horse racing a couple hours ago is headed for the ten dollar window.

Gymnastics fans are made in similar fashion. If you get to the meet early, you'll have time to study a program and then watch the gymnasts warm up. Both will help you handicap the meet. The warmup period generally begins at least twenty minutes before the scheduled starting time. And since the gymnasts have already completed most of their bending and stretching exercises at this point, you're likely to see them perform several tricks at full bore. The judges are not allowed to let any of this preliminary activity color their thinking, but the warmup period may give you some idea of who's hot and who's not. The program will prove invaluable, particularly in an international meet, because it should not only enable you to match names and countries with numbers and faces, but it should also include enough background on the competitors to give you an idea of who has a chance to win. To make some sense out of the meet, you should pick out several gymnasts, the actual number depending upon how many events are running at once, and follow them throughout the six events.

Let's say you have tickets to the 1979 Dial-American Cup, an international meet held at Madison Square Garden in New York. This is the first live gymnastics meet you have ever attended, and you are wondering how to figure out what's going on. Just from looking at the silver-colored souvenir program with the picture of Kurt Thomas on the cover, you could have picked up the following information:

• Compulsory exercises (which are only slightly more exciting than watching a skater trace circles in the ice) would not be competed at the American Cup, only optionals—thus more pizzazz.

• Though favored to win in the team competition at the 1980 Olympics in Moscow, the Soviet Union had sent two young gymnasts to New York whose reputations were such a mystery that, unlike the rest of the field, no bio sketch appeared after either one's name.

• Included in the field were three gold medalists from the recent World Championships in Strasbourg, France: Junichi Shimizu of Japan (vault), Zoltan Magyar of Hungary (pommel horse), and Thomas of the United States (floor exercise). Also present were two Olympic medal winners from the 1976 Games in Montreal: Henry Boerio of France (bronze medal, high bar) and Magyar (gold medal, pommel horse).

• Thomas, who had swept all six events in winning the 1978 American Cup, was fresh from a second-place finish in the All-Around competition at the World Cup in Sao Paulo, Brazil—a field that included nearly all of the men to beat in Moscow.

Armed with this information and the vision of how fit Thomas looked in the warmups, drawing an early round of applause from the crowd of 13,844 for a quick series of high-bounding somersaults, most anyone at the Garden that Sunday afternoon could have picked him as the man to beat in this meet. However, to have stayed abreast of Thomas's progress against Magyar, Shimizu, Boerio, and the rest of the field throughout the course of six events, you would have needed to do some additional homework beforehand.

To those millions of people who can't even balance their checkbooks, gymnastics math—wherein athletes' scores are broken down into tenths, hundredths, and even thousandths of a point—is incomprehensible. For example, after four events of the American Cup, Thomas had moved ahead of one of the two mystery Russians, Bogdan Makuts, by a score of 38.60 to 38.10. Was Thomas enjoying a comfortable lead or was he hanging on by the skin of his teeth? Most people at the Garden that day couldn't have told you, except many would have guessed from the closeness of the numbers that the meet must also be extremely close. Ask the same people to evaluate a baseball game in which the Yankees are leading the Red Sox 6–1 after six innings and every one of them could tell you the Yankees are enjoying a comfortable lead.

Therein lies the secret to evaluating how the leaders stand in a gymnastics meet: Treat .1 as the equivalent of one run in a baseball game. Thus, Thomas's .5 lead over Makuts ($38.60 - 38.10 = .5$) in a meet two-thirds of the way over is tantamount to the Yankees' five-run lead over the Red Sox after six innings. Remember, don't worry about the total scores; concentrate on the difference between one gymnast's score and another's. However, if you need to convince yourself that .5 represents a substantial lead for a gymnast of Thomas's

98

Thomas was also the first gymnast to incorporate the Flair into a floor exercise.

At important meets like the Olympics or World Championships a spectator cannot follow all the action, with six events going on at once. (*overleaf*)

caliber to maintain through two more events, do some quick division. If, after four events, Thomas's average score per event was 9.65 ($38.60 \div 4 = 9.65$) as compared to 9.525 for Makuts, he would really have to fall on his face in order to squander a .5 lead in the space of two events.

Gaining some idea of how a gymnast scores points, loses points, and gains some back again all in the course of one exercise is essential if you want to make like a real fan and start second-guessing the judges. First of all, do not assume that as a man prepares to begin his exercise, his reward for a perfectly executed routine will necessarily be a score of 10.0. Men must go to greater lengths than women to produce big numbers from the judges because the men's scoring system is more in step with the abilities of today's gymnasts. The women are judged against a five-part list of performance requirements, each with its own assigned numerical value, that adds up to 10.0. Satisfy all five parts completely and you get a 10.0. Nadia Comaneci did it seven times in the Montreal Olympics, and Nelli Kim twice more. Men, by design, almost never score 10.0. They receive points in three different categories—*difficulty* (3.4), *execution* (4.4), and *combination* (1.6)—whose numerical values add up to only 9.4. By the letter of the law, that's the best a man can do: 9.4. To score higher, he must give such an extraordinary performance that he qualifies for bonus points in the areas of *risk* (.2), *originality* (.2) and *virtuosity* (.2), commonly referred to in the trade as ROV.

While *difficulty* refers to the overall technical level of one's routine, *risk* refers to individual moves which the gymnast undertakes with the knowledge that they could work to his disadvantage just as easily as they could to his advantage. In the mind of a judge, he has programed danger into his exercise. For example, a Veronin is a move in which a gymnast releases his hold on the high bar, soars over the top, and catches the bar again on the other side. Doing it will help a gymnast's difficulty score. However, if he opens up his

legs on the way over the bar (called a straddle Veronin), causing his body to gain another foot of altitude and making the catch much more precarious, he might also receive .2 for risk.

Originality speaks for itself, although this is a fickle reward system that changes with the times. Once upon a time a Tsukahara vault was considered too difficult for most gymnasts to master. It consists of a side handspring up to the apparatus, followed by a back somersault down to the mat. Those few who could do it, including its inventor, Mitsuo Tsukahara of Japan, received originality points. Very few gymnasts use the original Tsukahara these days either, but the reason has nothing to do with difficulty. It has become so passé over the years that high school kids now use it. Which is why you must keep updating your tricks. Otherwise, you not only won't earn originality points, you'll hurt your difficulty score as well.

The Code of Points compares *virtuosity* in a gymnastics routine to the performance of a musician whose "brilliance rises above the level of technical accomplishment and so deeply impresses us that our souls are moved." Gymnasts say virtuosity merely means taking every move to the max. At any rate, getting credit for virtuosity is a lot harder than for risk or originality. A gymnast must show extreme form, height, or beauty and bring it off in such an apparently effortless manner that it looks as if someone else is doing the breathing, swinging, and lifting for him.

Rather than cluing them in on how to keep score right along with the judges, this little discussion on point-getting will convince many that scoring should be left to the men in the coats and ties. Not so. The fan in the stands can come surprisingly close to the score the judges arrive at just by watching a lot of gymnastics. It also helps to be aware of how a gymnast loses points with the judges. Here are some general rules of thumb:

• For walking in handstand or for landings or dis-

mounts that aren't stuck, each step means *.1 off.*
• A gymnast is supposed to project a tight body at
all times during a routine, with toes pointed and
everything else shipshape and ready for inspection.
Thus, little breaks in form such as bent arms on
parallel bars or saggy legs on pommel horse mean
.1 to .3 off.
• Moving rings or, on any strength move, any wobble
or failure to reach a vertical, depending on how
dramatic, means *.1 to .3 off.*
• Any stops on high bar or pommel horse, depending on how long, mean *.1 to .3 off.*
• Failure to hold a strength move—such as a handstand on floor—for two seconds means *.2 off.*
• Touching one's hands to the floor, without support, to regain balance on any landing or dismount
means *.3 off.*
• Using the hands as a means of support to prevent
what otherwise would be a fall means *.5 off.*
• Falling off the apparatus, be it pommel horse,
rings, parallel bars, or high bar, means *.5 off.*

Do not be surprised when a gymnast who has fallen
off an apparatus in the midst of his routine doesn't hop
back on in a frenzy or quit on the spot. Instead, he
will usually walk (with apparent calm) back to the
chalk pit, get a word of advice or encouragement from
his coach, signal the judges that he is ready to compete
again, and then pick up his routine at the point where
he left off. According to the rules, a fallen gymnast
has thirty seconds to recover—mentally as well as
physically—before completing his routine. During those
thirty seconds, he may cry, wave to his girl friend, or
have a little conversation with God. But regardless of
his personality or abilities, you can bank on the fact
that every guy who falls off will persevere and finish.
Keep in mind that with ROV, there is always the
chance he can gain back all or part of the .5 deduction
he just suffered.

A cram course in the vagaries of judging won't add

much to the enjoyment of your first meet, because
judging is a highly subjective occupation and personalities definitely enter into it. Why else would the
high and low scores be thrown out every time and the
two middle scores averaged? Keep in mind, too, that
if the meet is co-ed and the fields are of similar
strength, the women's scores should be higher than the
men's. In Montreal, in the finals of the women's
Olympic All-Around, the judges awarded twenty-seven
scores of 9.8 or higher. On the men's side, there were
eight. The discrepancy was even more dramatic, considering that just as many men competed as women
(thirty-six) and that the men's program consists of
two more events. Nadia and Nelli were both spectacular and gave truly unprecedented performances. Yet the
main reason the women's judges awarded so many
10.0s is that they rewarded too many early routines
that were merely "good" with 9.8s and 9.9s. When
something much better came along, they had painted
themselves into a corner. Mindful of this, men's judges
will consciously hold back scores for the first few
competitors up on an apparatus. So much so, that the
order in which a gymnast competes in relation to his
competitors is considered a significant factor in how he
scores.

Assuming you have finished your handicapping in
time to watch the first event, here is an additional word
of caution about format. If six events are to be run
simultaneously, you are in big trouble. That would
only be the case if the field were so large it necessitated
splitting the gymnasts up into six different flights with
each flight starting on a different apparatus. In which
case, while you are anticipating Gymnast A's dismount
on rings, you miss Gymnast B's vault. As you wait to
see what Gymnast B got from the judges, you miss
Gymnast A's score on the rings. When a 9.9 score is
flashed over at the high bar, you stand up to see what
the roar is all about and, in the process, miss B's vault
score, too. It's exciting, but confusing. Why else do you
think the TV networks show nothing but videotaped

gymnastics shows? Doing a live telecast would be complete chaos. If you're smart, you'll bring along a friend or two to act as spotters. You, alone, can probably follow only three gymnasts. If the format calls for only three events to be run at once, you might be able to follow six.

At the American Cup, the public address announcer came on just before the start of the first event to remind everyone that the standard Olympic program would be followed in order—floor exercise, pommel horse, rings, vault, parallel bars, high bar—and that with only seventeen gymnasts entered, the events would be conducted one at a time. Thus, you could probably have kept track of all seventeen, if you so desired, without even contracting a headache.

Lest it sound like the fans have the hardest task at a gymnastics meet, it should be remembered that for an All-Arounder like Kurt Thomas, every competition is a mini decathlon. Except that instead of having ten track and field events spread over two days, a gymnast must tackle six unforgiving apparatus in the space of two hours. Adding to the problem is the fact that, unlike the decathlon, where an athlete is given several chances to improve upon his initial mark in, say, the discus or high jump, a gymnast is accorded no second chances, no second opportunity to top what the other guy has scored. In working the six apparatus, a gymnast spends approximately four minutes' total time in front of the judges, so every little mistake is costly. You have to be something of a masochist to go in for this kind of pressure. But if the six events have any compensatory quality, it is that they have more in common with each other, as far as the athletic skills necessary to master them, than the shotput and the 100-meter hurdles do.

FLOOR EXERCISE. The most basic of the six events and the only one that doesn't involve an apparatus—other than a mat 1½ inches thick—floor exercise is a source for most of the movements and disciplines found in the other events. It's a scary way to start out, because the judges want to see everything you've got—tumbling, balance, strength, jumps, control, tricks, technique, flexibility, flips—the works. And as Kurt says, "You've got nothing to hold onto out there but air." The floor-ex mat measures 12 meters by 12 meters, about twice the dimensions of a boxing ring. Within those perimeters a gymnast must do multiple somersaults, getting head-high off the mat if he wants to please the judges. He must also land softly and with little or no staggering, for fear of stepping over the white boundary line and being assessed up to a .3 penalty.

Men's floor-ex is almost a different event from the more familiar women's version. Men's events are judged only by men, most of whom are former gymnasts. And while they appreciate showmanship, they want the ballet left to Baryshnikov as well as any musical accompaniment—even the background variety. That, horror of horrors, might suggest choreography. In contrast to the dance-oriented sequences associated with Olga and Nadia, this is a brazen display of tumbling, power, explosive speed, and raw athletic ability. The men must make four major passes across the mat (the women only two), with the first and fourth, referred to as the "mount" and "dismount," containing the most impressive sequence of tricks. In between, they will use the sidelines and the corners for their strength and balance parts.

As is the case with much of gymnastics, personal taste dictates who likes what in whom, and that goes for spectators as well as judges. For some, women's floor exercise is worth the price of admission all by itself because the contestants use the pulse of the music to play to the crowd, while mixing in enough modern dance to break the monotony of flips, flips, flips. Others find that a never-ending series of pixies, each one intent upon stealing your heart, becomes tiresome after a while. Men's floor-ex divides people in the same way, between those who find it unduly

macho and lacking in soul and those who are awed by the pyrotechnics. Judges prefer twisting somersaults to the regular everyday kind, which means a gymnast's body must spin laterally around its own axis like a top at the same time it is flipping end over end. Position of the legs in flight is also a crucial factor in the awarding of points. If a man does a somersault with his legs tucked up tight against his stomach, his score won't be as high as if he uses the "pike" position, where the body opens out into an L-shape as it rotates, or the exceedingly difficult "layout" position, in which the gymnast turns end over end in the same straight-body position that he assumes during walking.

The big tumbling passes you see, replete with Arabian cartwheels, sideways somersaults, and double back somersaults with a full twist, must be accomplished with a runup of no more than three steps, or else a penalty of up to .3 is incurred. The bell or gong that sounds near the end of the gymnast's routine is a signal from the otherwise unobtrusive judges that the exercise has passed the minimum length of time, fifty seconds, and that only twenty seconds remain before the maximum of seventy is reached.

Watch floor exercise carefully, because it is generally a showcase for a man's overall gymnastic abilities and an indication of how he will fare in the All-Around. This is not to say that a good gymnast won't do better in some other event, only that if a gymnast is bad on floor he probably won't be much of a threat in the All-Around. If he wobbles on the way up to his hand-stand or can't hold it for a full two seconds, he probably lacks the strength and control necessary to excel on rings and parallel bars. Does he get head-high on his somersaults and can he stick his landings and dismount? If so, chances are he's a good vaulter, too.

The most important facet of a floor exercise routine is the ability to pull off the big tricks, thereby setting yourself apart from the rest of the crowd. Andrianov is known for his double back somersaults in the layout position. And now, following his gold-medal-winning performance in Strasbourg, Thomas has gained a reputation for something besides his Flair—the 1½ twisting, 1¾ somersault.

To make the trick work, Thomas has to build up enough momentum in the space of just a few feet to propel his body eight feet off the mat. But that's only the beginning of his problems. While he is initiating the twisting movement that will cause his body to rotate 1½ times around its own axis, he must also start tucking himself into a ball for the 1¾ somersault he performs at the same time. That means he will be stopping just short of two somersaults—landing on his back and continuing into a forward roll, rather than turning another quarter revolution in the air and landing in conventional fashion on his feet. With such a hair-raising ending in mind, Thomas must gauge the trick perfectly right from the beginning. He must achieve the proper height and have just the right air time and angle of descent. If he comes down short, he ends up on his nose; if he lands on his neck when he hits the mat, he might break a cervical vertebra. It wouldn't be the first time it has happened to Thomas.

The rest of Thomas's routine in Strasbourg was also crammed with difficulty. After his big opener, he bounded into an Arabian dive roll, again landing on his back but rolling out into a slow, methodical straddle press to a handstand. Continuing to support his entire body on his hands, he showed superb strength and control by lowering both legs behind him, then pulling them between his arms and out in front of him (called a stoop through), continuing on up to a high V-seat with both legs together and toes pointed toward the ceiling. For good measure, Kurt then did the entire move in reverse, eventually resuming the hand-stand position. His third pass across the mat ended with a very concise double back somersault tucked up nicely and stuck tight. Next came his Thomas Flair on the floor, a remarkable physical feat since he again supports himself solely on his hands, then splays his legs high and low—making circles above his head and

Three varieties of somersaults in increasing order of difficulty. In the customary "tucked" position at left, the gymnast bends his knees and pulls his legs up against his chest. In the "piked" position the legs are kept straight and away from the body, forming an L-shape. In the "layout" position, a gymnast flips end over end in relatively the same straight-body position he assumes during walking.

Scissors are an integral part of every pommel horse routine. The gymnast straddles the horse, swings one leg high out over the end and then, in pendulum fashion, sweeps back and swings the other leg high above the opposite end.

Miroslav Cerar of Yugoslavia displayed perfect form—legs straight and together, toes pointed—in winning a gold medal on pommel horse at the 1964 Olympics in Tokyo. From 1962 to 1968 he was the best in the world on the horse.

Zoltan Magyar of Hungary has dominated the pommel horse event as long as Cerar did. He was Olympic champion in 1976 and has won gold medals in the last three World Championships.

around his body—without stubbing his feet on the mat. It is a very unusual move, almost as innovative as Tsukahara's original vault that stunned the gymnastics world. To wrap up the gold medal, Thomas needed only to hit a "double twister," a back somersault with two twists. He nailed it and the crowd loved it. But most of them were still buzzing about his 1½ twisting, 1¾ somersault. The move looks as difficult as it sounds, and if you don't know what's coming ahead of time, the ending is as surprising as one of Hitchcock's.

POMMEL HORSE. Dead last in potential danger, aesthetic movements, spectacular dismounts, and big numbers from the judges, the pommel horse is easily the most moribund event on the program. Not many people like it—and that includes the competitors. In fact, coming on the heels of all those high-voltage floor-ex routines, the start of the horse competition is usually a time when spectators slip out for popcorn and Cokes. What they miss, however, is the most difficult of the six events. Particularly in terms of making the moves look easy, which is the desired end of every gymnastics routine.

The physical nature of this event—asking a man to support all his weight on his hands while he swings his legs around and around in lateral circles, thus interfering with his hands' support position every half-second or so—seems to ask the impossible. The rules say movement must be continuous, but that is more a piece of friendly advice than an admonishment. When a gymnast loses momentum on pommel horse, the legs have a tendency to bend, the body sags, and the entire routine can grind to a halt right there in the saddle of the horse. Or, worse yet, on the floor beside it.

The secret to survival on the horse, or so most gymnasts say, is balance. Keep it, and one's initial swinging movements will carry him through the entire routine. True enough, although oversimplified and a bit optimistic. Another key ingredient is rhythm, as well as a certain affinity for the apparatus. Kurt Thomas

agrees. "That's a big part of it. If you just naturally feel what tempo you need to keep your body in sync with the progression of your routine, it's a lot simpler than trying to think to yourself, 'Grip, swing, release, catch! Grip, swing, release, catch!' about twenty times a routine."

In the end, all most pommel-horse competitors care about is stayin' alive. However, the judges are looking for something more. Besides the double leg circles which are the foundation of every routine, a gymnast must include a pair of "scissors," wherein he straddles the apparatus and in pendulum fashion swings one leg high over the end of the horse, then drops down and swings the other leg high over the other end. If at the height of his scissors, his elevated hip is as high as his opposite shoulder—the one giving support—then he is probably earning top points. There are few other prerequisites, other than working all parts of the horse, including both ends, and showing support with the hands behind the back at some point in the routine. The rest has been left up to the gymnasts, whose collective imagination had failed until recently to produce any tricks that could compete with popcorn and Cokes. Now there are at least two.

The Magyar Spindle is really an entire sequence of moves which the Hungarian Olympic champion Zoltan Magyar has been doing, without imitation, since the mid-1970s and for which he invariably receives .2 in originality points. The Spindle was designed to show sophisticated use of one end of the horse, and to Magyar's credit, it is an impressive display of hand positioning and body manipulation done amid a series of lightning-fast leg circles. To the layman, however, it looks as though Magyar were trying to put out a fire with his hands. Technically speaking, it's beautiful; visually, it's not. But then, what is on the horse?

For the moment, only the Thomas Flair. But these sweeping, airborne leg twirls represent such a departure that some judges feel Thomas may have liberated the horse just as Italy's Franco Menicelli did

with floor exercise back in the 1960s when he started
the trend away from strength moves and posing.
However great a role it plays in inspiring gymnasts of
the future to develop new and daring pommel-horse
tricks, the Flair is so popular and so easy to do—in
comparison to the Spindle—that it is not likely to
provide Thomas with the kind of longevity in originality points that Magyar has gotten out of his
invention. The more success your competitors have in
copying your move, the less likely you are to keep
getting originality points for it. Unless, of course, you
continue to add new wrinkles as Thomas has done with
a second Flair which he performs on the opposite side
of the horse so the people on the other side of the
arena can get a good look at it. The Tsukahara vault
hasn't exactly been put in mothballs either. With the
addition of a full twist or a piked somersault, it is
being competed in an updated form and still evokes
good scores from the judges.

If only something could be done about those
woebegone pommel horse dismounts. With no chance
to gain the leverage that one has on an apparatus like
the parallel bars, pommel horse competitors finish their
routines by simply *getting off*. Don't look for any flips
or even a simple twist, because it's next to impossible
to get that much lift. The standard dismount is a maneuver called a loop with a half-twist, in which the
gymnast merely pushes up and away from the apparatus
with his hands. The higher his seat and legs go, the
better his score, providing that form is good. Look for
pommel horse scores to be lower, on the average, than
those on any other event. In the All-Around competition in Strasbourg, the scores on horse averaged 9.23,
lagging .2 behind the next lowest scoring event.

RINGS. Strictly an event for blacksmiths back
when every routine was crammed full of strength moves
called crosses, the rings has become much more elegant
to watch because the emphasis has changed to include
more swinging parts. Those frozen midair poses, com-

plete with bulging muscles and steel-eyed stares, are
still around and still a big favorite with the crowd. But
nowadays, you're likely to see rings routines which are
as much as 65 percent fluid motion.

This isn't to imply that rings is an event gymnasts
look forward to. It is still the most physically taxing of
the six events, as you can tell by listening to the names
of some of the moves: iron cross, hanging scale and,
the worst-sounding one of all, the dislocate. But with
the advent of swing, 126-pounders like Thomas have
a real chance to do what they could not have done
with judging conducted the way it was back in the
1950s—that is, score as well on rings as a muscle man
like Andrianov. To do so, a gymnast must learn the
knack of using the potential energy present in the ten
feet of cable between the rings and the top of the
apparatus to propel himself up, around, and down
again in a quicksilver manner that strength alone could
never muster. To a physicist or an auto mechanic, this
action would be called "torque," not swing. But no
matter.

The rings is basically a stop-and-go event, with
judges looking for a gymnast to alternate his swing,
strength and hold parts. However, of the two handstands required, only one has to be done via pure
strength—called "pressing a handstand." The other can
be what's called a shoot ("swing") to a handstand. In
addition, every routine has to include one of those
old-time crowd-pleasers, a cross—be it the Maltese,
iron, or Olympic variety—or a close relative such as a
lever or a planche. This is one area where swing can't
do a thing for you; you need pure strength.

Technically speaking, the rings event is known as the
still rings. And for a very good reason: Rings can swing
the gymnast, but the gymnast must not swing the
rings, or else he loses points with the judges. Lest this
sound impossible, try to watch the event from the side
sometime so that, as a gymnast is being held aloft by
his coach at the start of his routine, you are looking
at his profile. From there, a good rings man can rise

The rings are located more than eight feet off the mat, so most gymnasts need a boost up. As soon as Roger Counsil is sure that Thomas has a good grip and that the rings are perfectly still, he moves away. Moments later, Thomas maneuvers into an L-cross.

The most easily recognized trick in gymnastics—the iron cross—performed here by Eizo Kenmotsu of Japan.
A back lever

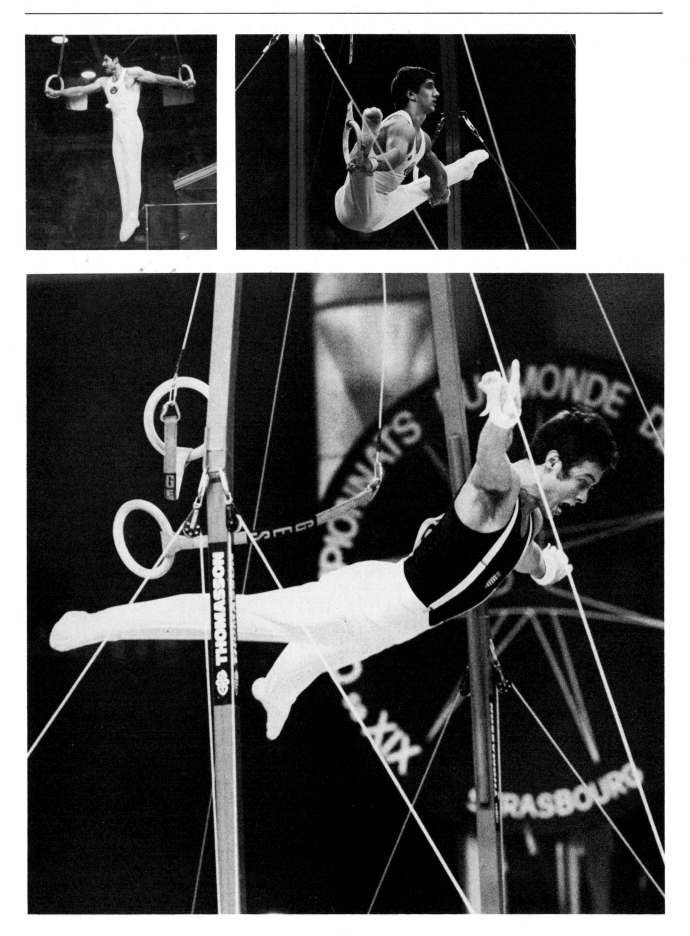

to a support position, press to a handstand, swing back up to another handstand, and all the while the cables should barely be visible to you because they will be hidden by the outside framework of the apparatus. It's when the rings start to swing back and forth—or left and right of the frame as you look at it from the side—that you realize a gymnast is losing control.

What is a "dislocate," and how long does it take to heal? Actually, this painful-sounding term stands for a simple rotational movement well within the physical capabilities of anyone who has a healthy ball-and-socket joint in his shoulder. On this event, it's the least of a gymnast's worries.

VAULT. The vault is performed on the "long horse," essentially a pommel horse without pommels. A gymnast sprints toward the long horse at top speed, lands on a little springboard with both feet, and is catapulted onto either the near or far end of the apparatus, which he meets with his hands. At this point, the gymnast pushes himself up, up, and away into one of the fifty-two different vaults listed in the Code of Points.

The difficulty in the vaulting event is not in mastering the apparatus. Although the long horse does provide most of the height of the vault, and not the springboard as you might guess, it is more or less a neutral surface between a sixty-six-foot runup and a hairbreadth landing. The real difficulty lies in knowing when to untuck or unpike from your somersault or handspring when you've built up sixty-six feet of speed —not just three steps' worth, as in floor exercise. The problem then gets passed along to the landing, which has to be just right or else you end up running, sliding, or bounding off the end of the mat and out into the parking lot.

Unlike the other five events, each of which must contain at least eleven separate moves of varying difficulty, the vault is a one-shot deal: a fancy dismount with no routine preceding it. Hence, it must be

evaluated and scored differently. Since it's over in just a few seconds, a judge scarcely has the time or the eyesight to break it down into eleven parts. Instead, every one of those fifty-two vaults in the Code of Points has been assigned what in diving vernacular would be called a degree of difficulty. The ratings range from 7.0 to 9.8, and they represent the maximum score a gymnast can attain for performing that particular vault perfectly. In this case, the judges have withheld only .2 in virtuosity points which they can award for an exemplary effort. The risk and originality factors have already been taken into account in the vault's rating. For example, the old Tsukahara in the tuck position has been devalued to 9.4. But the updated versions in the pike position or with a full twist added are rated at 9.8.

To be a good vaulter, you must possess track and field talents as well, because in recent years the event has gotten to be one-third high jump, one-third trick, and one-third long jump, at least in the minds of some judges. That isn't strictly true, because if you mess up your tumbling move it won't matter how high or how far you vaulted. Nevertheless, a good vault must have great height and distance, so add sprinting as a necessary skill. The only way to achieve height above the apparatus and distance down the mat after contact is with great speed on the runup. By the way, although a gymnast isn't graded on his runup, it is considered part of the vault. Once he blasts off, he can't abort before takeoff.

While judges can't carve up a vault into eleven different parts, they do check for some fairly esoteric data, including whether a gymnast's seat reaches a height above the long horse equal to four-fifths of the length of the horse. This is another reason the fan has a difficult time participating in the judging process. On the other hand, the vault provides a wonderful opportunity for the sport of gymnastics to involve people in the stands with what is going on down on the floor. Before each man prepares to do his vault, he could turn

A handspring vault by Alexander Ditiatin of the Soviet Union

over a larger flip card that would flash the name of the vault and its degree of difficulty to the crowd. That would not only begin to chip away at the jargon problem, it would also provide that badly-needed mental reference point. Here's what would happen:

As Gymnast A gets ready for his vault, a sign that reads "Tsukahara, pike (9.8)" is flashed to the crowd. Gymnast A takes off and really nails it, taking everything to the max and sticking his dismount. The judges give him a 9.65. A few people in the audience whistle, but no one seems terribly upset. Next up is Gymnast B, an Olympic champion in the vault and the current leader in the All-Around standings after three events. Again the sign flashes "Tsukahara, pike (9.8)," and a little drama begins to develop. Gymnast B shows a lot of athleticism in his Tsukahara, getting extremely high over the apparatus. But he doesn't look as smooth as Gymnast A and he takes a little hop after his landing. When the judges give him a 9.8, everybody in the arena is *involved*. A conference is called; one judge looks rather sheepish, another is mad. Now the crowd has someone to side with. And against.

This is what *could* happen, but generally does not. In fact, instead of flashing the name of the vault and its degree of difficulty to the crowd, meet directors confuse the issue even further. To notify the panel of judges what vault a gymnast intends to do, most meet directors utilize a flip card with a code number on it—such as number 17. The judge then looks in his Code of Points and sees that number 17 stands for a Tsukahara vault in the pike position. The people who bought $8.50 tickets hoping to get an inside look at gymnastics are told nothing. They go home singing the praises of that number 17 vault Gymnast A did and are more confused than ever by all the numbers.

PARALLEL BARS. If floor exercise is characterized as the universal donor of gymnastics, in that the event requires movements and physical disciplines which, once learned, can be passed on to the other five events, the parallel bars is the universal recipient. The parallel bars event is so derivative in nature that most gymnasts do p-bar routines that look like a Greatest Hits of their other five exercises. On these two stationary bars, which are 11½ feet long and anchored 5½ feet off the ground, you may see double leg circles —ordinarily the stock and trade of the pommel horse— as well as front flips and handstands from floor-ex, L-supports from rings, a giant swing from high bar, and some daredevilish twisting dismounts reminiscent of the vault.

Part of the reason this event offers a gymnast so much flexibility is that it also offers him more physical security than any other event. The bars provide any number of places to hold on and they are also flexible, an equipment change which has occurred over the years in keeping with a shift in concept similar to what is happening on the rings. No longer a platform for handstand after handstand, these new fiberglass bars now enable gymnasts to soar above the apparatus and perform somersaults. Ideally, p-bar routines should consist of equal parts swing, flight, and hold, and contain no more than three stops. In the All-Around competition, judges expect to see a release and recatch when the body is below the bars as well as when it is above them.

If you're trying to sniff out ROV points, watch for unusual mounts. Most gymnasts walk slowly to the end of the bars and begin their routine with a nondescript swing to a support position. Thomas starts from the middle on one side, dives underneath both bars and catches hold on the opposite side, then rises to a V-seat. Magyar places a vaulting board at the end of the bars and somersaults into a support position. Anything, it seems, is possible as long as you have the imagination to dream it up and the talent to carry it off. The feeling in gymnastics circles is that parallel bar routines will change more in the next ten years than any others.

A practice vault where a gymnast tries to assess his speed and timing.

What the approach, or "preflight" segment, of a handspring front looks like.

The preflight for a Tsukahara with a full twist

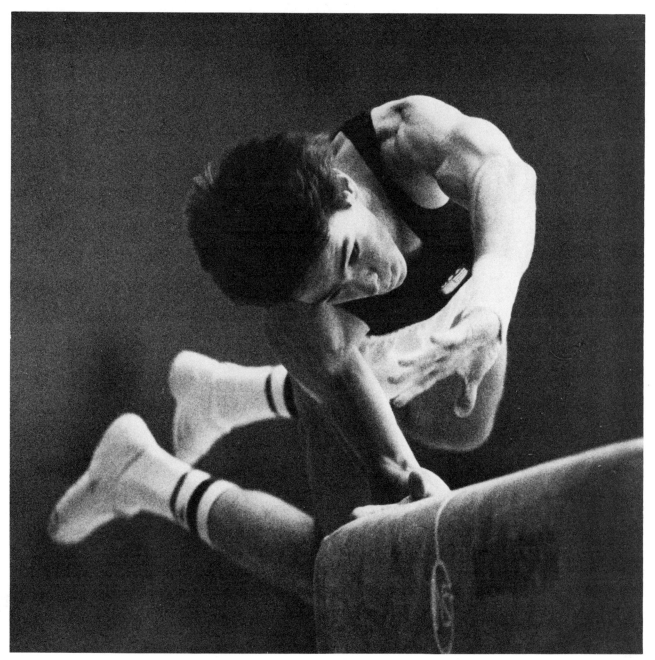

The front uprise on parallel bars is usually a prelude to a more difficult move. The swing forward creates potential energy and gets Peter Kormann ready for his dismount.

A back toss, in which a gymnast flips backward from one handstand to another.

Most gymnasts mount the parallel bars slowly and unspectacularly from one end. Thomas dives underneath both bars and grabs the middle of the bar that's farthest from him. He then rises to a straddle press or a V-seat.

Stoyan Deltchev zips around the high bar in the back Stalder position.

German giants, such as these by Mike Wilson, require tremendous flexibility.

Nikolai Andrianov using one of his favorite floor-exercise maneuvers, the double-layout somersault, as a dismount from the high bar.

A straddle Veronin on high bar, accomplished by letting go of the bar after a giant swing, kicking open the legs while soaring over the top, then recatching when you come down on the other side of the bar.

Shinzo Shiraishi of Japan tucks his legs inside his arms on a stoop-in.

HIGH BAR. The closest thing to the circus that the world of sport has to offer, the high-bar competition is staged last for a very good reason: It would upstage any event that came afterward. What we have here is the aesthetic opposite of the horse; everything on high bar looks exciting. Once you see Thomas soar fourteen feet above the floor on his front 1¼ somersault, or Andrianov dismount with a triple back somersault, it's impossible not to think of the trapeze. Something else high bar routines make you think of is the childhood fear of sailing over the top of the swing set. Except these guys get so used to sailing over the top of the bar they don't think a thing of it. Some fun they'd be on a roller coaster.

Since high bar exercises can have no stops whatsoever, each competitor must push himself hard from beginning to end. That adds to an already existing drama, because, as this last event on the program begins, something big is almost always at stake, whether it is a high school ribbon, a college dual meet, an NCAA title, a trip overseas, a world championship, or an Olympic medal. In an All-Around competition such as the American Cup, this may be the first time all day that your scorekeeping has really made sense to you. With some simple arithmetic, you can now figure out exactly what it will take for a gymnast to overtake the man in front of him. Earlier in the meet, those figures could have been somewhat deceptive.

Thomas's .5 lead over Makuts after four events was a comfortable lead all right, but not just because of the raw numbers. What made his margin even safer was the fact that the two world champions, Shimizu and Magyar, had already completed their strongest events. Shimizu had won the vault with a score of 9.6 and Magyar had taken the horse with a 9.75, but both events were behind them and they stood no better than third and fourth in the standings. If their best events had been in front of them, Thomas's lead would have meant less than the actual numbers seemed to indicate.

Thomas increased his lead over Makuts to .6 with a 9.7 on parallel bars, and as the high bar got underway, very little was actually at stake. Makuts went first and turned in a good-looking 9.7, but that meant Thomas had only to score higher than 9.1 to win. Having scored 9.8 on high bar in the preliminaries the day before, Thomas knew he could probably afford to fall completely off the apparatus, take the .5 deduction, and still walk away with the meet. But he was taking no chances. "I'm playing it safe," he said before he went up. And for him, he was, although the only place you might have noticed it was on his Veronin, which was rather flat and undistinguished. The judges didn't seem to mind, as they frequently don't when the leader in the All-Around is the last one up in the meet. They gave him a 9.8 and sent all 13,844 spectators home extremely happy.

131

Judging

Gymnastics is a sport. But International Gymnastics is more like an insidious parlor game which combines the treachery of *Battleship* with the ingenuity of *Monopoly*. To play, you must maneuver your national team through a maze of six different events while judges from enemy countries try to sink as many of your gymnasts as they can. For your country to win medals, it helps to make deals and arrange for "tradeoffs" beforehand so when one of your gymnasts lands on an event where an unfriendly judge is seated he won't get burned too badly. But beware of double crosses! Some countries ask for favors but don't reciprocate. The most popular strategy is to collaborate with only those nations whose political persuasions are similar enough to yours that you can count on them for aid. As for the countries you can't bargain with, you watch their judges very, very closely. If they begin destroying your team, you order your judges to take retaliatory action.

Almost everyone plays the game this way, but the Russians—and the satellite countries they control—are the masters. They used the same kind of chicanery to get a Russian in as president of the Federation Internationale de Gymnastique and to control the powerful FIG Technical Committee, which makes all the important judging decisions and in effect runs the sport. The United States, meantime, just stands around grumbling about the impropriety of it all and leading cheers against the Soviet Union. To play the game or not, that is the question which paralyzes the Americans. Do they act like the Russians (perish the thought!) or try to emulate the Japanese, whose Samurai-like proficiency in gymnastics has allowed them to remain aloof to these Cold War-type squabbles between East and West?

This is not to say that international gymnastics meets are "fixed" in the same sense that college basketball games in the United States during the 1950s were fixed. But with all the point-shaving (and point-gouging) that goes on in Europe, someone should have called in Scotland Yard a long time ago. The problem is usually referred to as a *scandal*, as in "the scandal of international judging," and it crops up all the time. Whenever a great deal of prestige is at stake (and even when it's not), judges from Eastern Bloc nations will try by whatever means are available to sabotage the endeavors of their country's athletic and political enemies. Sometimes their motives are purely personal, owing to a huge ego or fierce allegiance to the flag. But a few judges from Eastern Europe have admitted privately that they "deliver scores" in order to guarantee that their passport will be renewed.

What results is an unfortunate pentimento: The shiny, pristine image that gymnastics once projected can no longer mask a dark, seamy underside that the sport's hierarchy has been glossing over for years.

In what other sport could the rulemakers penalize an athlete .3 for throwing his grips in disgust at his own exercise, yet impose no sanctions against a Russian gymnastics official who stood up at an important international meeting and asked a group of judges to keep American and Japanese scores down. The man's name was Yuri Titov and he made his remarks at the 1974 World Championships in Varna, Bulgaria. Two years later, Titov was elected president of the FIG. What's more, he never denied the substance of those remarks. "Why should I," he has said, "when I know the United States and Canada were holding a meeting at the same time and for the same purpose?" Except that the U.S.-Canada conference Titov spoke of reportedly had nothing to do with the 1974 World Championships; the topic was Montreal and what could be done *within the rules* to prevent the kind of one-sided judging that had spoiled previous Olympics. Nobody made any concrete proposals, but some people began making plans for a counterattack, as Tom Zivic, a national coach in Canada, explains:

"The United States, Japan, and one or two other nations are the only ones who do not actively politic with other countries in order to get better scores. Unless the United States begins to press for favors in

When the pommel horse judge has decided on a score for Thomas's routine he will write it on a slip of paper and hand it to his assistant, the girl on the left. She then delivers it to the table where the superior judge sits. Through a complicated set of criteria, he computes the final score that is finally flashed to the crowd.

American judge Bob Stout
When a coach lodges an official protest over a gymnast's score, judges watch the routine over again on videotape.

return for other favors, it will never obtain the top positions which it merits. We in Canada have decided to begin collaborating with Hungary and Bulgaria. Why fight it?"

A tradeoff doesn't have to be a clandestine operation. On the contrary, some take place in the hotel coffee shop, at the bar, or during a trip to the men's room. More often than not, the arrangements are made closer to the action—at a judges' meeting, a practice session, or even while the meet is going on. The exchange is usually short and to the point, with the specifics of the conversation depending on where connections are needed and where they can be arranged. The negotiations involve judges and coaches, and sometimes even the gymnasts are approached, as Kurt Thomas can attest. At the 1977 World University Games in Sofia, Bulgaria, Thomas was warming up for floor exercise when the head judge on that event, a Romanian, walked over to him and said, "Look, talk to your American judge on rings for me. I'll get you in third place on floor if he takes care of our team on rings."

"I couldn't believe it," says Thomas. "It really shocked me. I knew that this sort of thing went on through coaches and judges, but I never knew they'd try to get the gymnasts involved."

In other words, when it comes down to the actual performance, winning a gold medal doesn't merely hinge upon all the sacrifices a gymnast makes—the six hours of practice every day, the null and void social life, the endless competitions, the exhaustive travel requirements, the pain and exertion—but also on the color of his flag, how much clout he carries with the judges, and whether he has enough talent to blast through what may be an Iron Curtain of prejudice.

The 16,000 people who had filled the Forum in Montreal to capacity sounded like a typical Tuesday night hockey crowd. They were a loud, foot-stomping bunch, the kind that usually turns out to see the Cana-

diens play the Boston Bruins. However, the entertainment on this night in July 1976 was not hockey, but Olympic gymnastics, specifically the finals of the men's team competition.

An upset of mammoth proportions was in the making. After two events a brash, young team from the Soviet Union was leading the grand old men of Japan. Not since the 1958 World Championships in Moscow had the Russians been able to defeat the Japanese, whose string of four Olympic team titles (1960–64–68–72) and four World Championship titles (1962–66–70–74) had in each case been accomplished at the expense of the second-place Soviets. In these two-part team competitions, the Japanese long suit had always been the compulsory exercises, where their extreme diligence and attention to basic form generally gave them a lead too big for the more adventuresome Soviets to overcome during the next night's optionals. But now the champions were in deep trouble. In Montreal, it was the USSR that led after the compulsories, 286.80 to 286.30. And when, on the second event of optional night, Alexander Ditiatin, Vladimir Markelov, and Nikolai Andrianov blistered the rings event with three 9.9s in a row, the old order seemed on its way out.

But as the teams rotated to the third event, Japan to the rings and the USSR to the vault, the advantage began to seesaw back and forth. Drawing on their experience in international waters and forgetting their age, which averaged out to twenty-seven years per man, the Japanese began chipping away at the Soviets' 1.1 lead. The opportunity was presented when two eighteen-year-old Russians messed up their vaults, scoring only 9.2 and 8.65. Shun Fujimoto answered with a 9.7 on rings, but on his dismount he aggravated an already painfully injured leg. As Fujimoto hobbled off the floor, unable to continue any further, his team faced a sobering fact: Japan would have to make its comeback with five men competing against six. According to the rules of gymnastics, only a team's top five scores are counted on each event—the lowest is thrown

Rings competition was the center of controversy in Montreal.

Yuri Titov, newly elected president of the *Federation Internationale de Gymnastique*. As one prominent American gymnastics official has said of Titov, "He's not such a bad man to have in charge, except that he can't forget for even one minute that he's a Russian."

Arthur Gander of Switzerland, former president of the FIG and a voice for sanity and impartiality in international gymnastics for thirty years

Boris Shakhlin of the USSR, the superior judge who got into a shoving match with Gander in Montreal

out. Thus, the Soviets could throw out their 8.65 score on vault and would continue to enjoy that luxury. With Fujimoto hurt, the Japanese would not.

The last man up on rings was Sawao Kato, who turned in a meticulous if unspectacular routine for which he was given a 9.8. The 16,000 spectators, most of whom were Americans and Canadians, would have none of it. The Russians' string of 9.9s was still on their minds and they whistled and booed for Kato to receive the same treatment. Spain's Enrique Gonzalez, the superior judge on rings, called for a conference with one of the four judges serving under him and asked the man if he would consider changing his score. The judge was Albert Azarian, a two-time Olympic gold medalist on rings from the USSR, and in light of the fact that Azarian had just finished giving several Russians a score of 10.0, Gonzalez didn't feel his request was too far out of line.

Azarian was as steadfast in his refusal as he used to be in holding a Maltese cross, and as his discussion with Gonzalez deteriorated into an argument, a lot of other people around the Forum were getting excited. Masao Takemoto, chief of the Japanese delegation, went to Arthur Gander, outgoing president of the FIG, and lodged a formal protest over Kato's score. The crowd, sensing it might be able to finish what it had started, was working itself into a higher state of frenzy. And Boris Shakhlin, the most decorated Olympic medalist the Soviet Union ever produced, was growing more and more impatient with the rings situation as he watched from his distant vantage point as superior judge on high bar.

Shakhlin should have been too busy tending to his own event to worry about what was happening elsewhere. But the look on his face gave him away: He didn't just want to beat the Japanese, he wanted every nickel. When Shakhlin could stand it no longer, he got up, walked the length of the floor, and pushed his way into the dispute between Azarian and Gonzalez. Interfering with the workings of another event is not

one of the powers granted to a superior judge, so that brought Gander out of his seat in the official FIG section and into the fracas. Gander had already made one trip down to the floor to chastise Azarian for those 10.0s he had given the Russian rings men. Now, as he moved to head off Shakhlin, he was anxious to put an end to this Kato business—and in no mood for a test of strength.

There they stood, nose-to-nose: Shakhlin, still virile in appearance though in his mid-forties, towering over the little white-haired man from Switzerland who had fought like a bulldog for nearly thirty years to bring fairness and sanity to international gymnastics. Then Shakhlin must have said something Gander didn't like. Most anything would have done it at that point, but Shakhlin probably made a remark about Gander being a lame duck president who shouldn't even be out on the floor. Whatever it was—neither man would say afterward—Gander turned bright red and gave Shakhlin a shove that might have landed him back at the high bar except for all the people in the way. From the stands, it looked like a hockey-style donnybrook might erupt. It didn't, mainly because Shakhlin and Gander had been barking at each other since the first time they met, sometimes in mortal anger and other times over a few late-night vodkas.

In the end, it was decided that Kato's 9.8 would stand. But when it came time to rotate to the next event, the noise in the arena was still so deafening that none of the gymnasts on the floor (East Germany, Hungary, and Romania were also trying to compete) could hear the signal. The entire incident took only five minutes, but it did as much damage to the Russians' momentum as a two-hour rain delay can do to a baseball pitcher's arm. Thereafter, the crowd cheered every move the Japanese made, which helped make up for the loss of Fujimoto and loosened up the judges considerably. Over the last three events, the Soviets managed only one score as high as 9.8, while the top Japanese men were ringing up two 9.8s, two

9.85s, and a 9.9. More importantly, the lowest Japanese score over the last three events—the one that had to be counted—came within .05 of what the fifth- and sixth-place Russians were able to muster. When Mitsuo Tsukahara whipped through a 9.9 routine as the last man up on high bar, the grand old men had beaten the Soviets for the ninth straight time.

Shakhlin's move had backfired. In winning the battle with Gander, he had lost the war, and that was doubly ironic because the stubborn old Swiss had been a thorn in Shakhlin's side before.

The 1962 World Championships were held in Prague at a time when Czechoslovakia was easing toward a period of more liberalized control from the Soviet Union, which may account for what took place during the finals of the parallel bars competition. Shakhlin, the 1960 Olympic champion in that event as well as in the All-Around, was pitted against Miroslav Cerar of Yugoslavia. Shakhlin went first and turned in his usual clean, strong routine. Cerar followed with an exercise of such elegance and inventiveness that U.S. coaches still marvel at films of it today. Watching it sixteen years later, one cannot imagine Cerar not getting the gold medal. And yet the judges gave him the same mark they had given Shakhlin. In a satellite country like Czechoslovakia, open hostility toward the Soviet Union is almost never expressed in the streets. But at sporting events the Russians are fair game, and in Prague that day the crowd really let the judges have it. The demonstration lasted nearly thirty minutes, and when it became apparent the noise wasn't going to subside until somebody looked into the matter, it· was Gander who intervened—this time against Shakhlin the competitor.

In 1962, Gander had not yet been elected president of the FIG, but he was chairman of the Technical Committee. He was the most influential man in the sport, and nobody questioned his presence on the floor of a meet. When Gander said his piece in Prague, the score was changed and Cerar was awarded the gold medal. Then as now, the Technical Committee was looked upon as the Supreme Court of gymnastics. Its seven members are reputed to be the seven finest judges in the world, men whose knowledge of the sport is unique and whose character is beyond reproach. When an international policy dispute arises, these men should be the most qualified to settle it, if necessary by a 4–3 vote. Their duties also include making and enforcing the rules, choosing sites for meets, assigning judges to competitions, and officiating at the World Championships and the Olympics—all the important things. Therefore, the political makeup of the committee has always determined which areas of the globe would benefit the most from its policy-making sessions. The TC has always been top-heavy with Eastern European members, but when Gander was chairman, from 1956 to 1972, his inbred notions of neutrality helped maintain a balance of power. From 1966, when he was also elected president of the FIG, until the 1972 Munich Olympics, all substantive matters crossed his desk before being resolved. However, in 1972, acting on the curious advice of friends, Gander gave up what for him was a more natural job as head of the Technical Committee to concentrate on his bureaucratic duties as FIG president. For four years, Ivan Ivancevic of Yugoslavia filled the position, then, in 1976, Alexander Lylo was made head of the TC. Lylo is a Czech citizen and a man of high principles, but he's not about to stand up to the Russians.

At a judges' meeting the day after the rings dispute in Montreal, Lylo stated that he had "not been satisfied with the judging." Marcel Adatte of Switzerland tried to take the issue further. "The problem of judging is a serious one and we can no longer tolerate the actions we have witnessed at these Games," he said. "Judges are collaborating with each other and deciding not only on scores but also on the distribution of medals." Adatte is normally a quiet, unassuming man. Yet here he was standing up at the Olympics making charges that, in essence, the meet was fixed!

A familiar scene over the years:
victorious Japanese accepting congratulations from second-place
Russians

The FIG Technical Committee is the Supreme Court of gymnastics. Its seven members are reputed to be the finest judges in the world and, in effect, they run the entire sport. The members include:

Akitomo Kaneko of Japan

Boris Shakhlin of the USSR

Karl Heinz Zschocke of East Germany

Sandor Urvary of Hungary

Tuomo Jalantie of Finland

Alexander Lylo of Czechoslovakia

Enrique Gonzalez of Spain

Having brought the issue up in the first place, Lylo now backed down. "This is not the time for such discussions," he said, and then proceeded with some innocuous announcements.

Lylo was right about it not being the proper time or place for a long harangue on judging, at least for his sake. If he had allowed debate on the Gander-Shakhlin dispute of the previous evening, the assembly might have become intrigued with something else Adatte said before he relinquished the microphone: "I regret to say that some of the members of the Technical Committee are guilty of the offenses of which I speak."

In global terms, four of the TC members are within driving distance of each other. Lylo, the chairman, is from Czechoslovakia; then there is Karl Heinz Zschocke of East Germany, Sandor Urvary of Hungary, and Shakhlin of the Soviet Union. Since these four members invariably vote together, in terms of decision-making it isn't terribly important what the other three members think. They can either support the preexisting majority opinion or go out and bang their heads against the wall. For the record, they are: Tuomo Jalantie of Finland, whose country did not qualify a single competitor for the Montreal Games; Akitomo Kaneko of Japan, whose technical expertise helped artists draw the moves included in the Code of Points; and Spain's Enrique Gonzalez, who tangled with Shakhlin and Azarian on the floor of the Forum. Throw in FIG President Titov, the Russian who made a name for himself in Varna, and you have a rather one-sided lineup. Not only does it leave out the entire Western Hemisphere, it also excludes the country with perhaps the strongest, most conscientious judging organization in the world, namely the United States. The fact that the United States Gymnastics Federation contributed most of the money which kept the FIG afloat from 1966 to 1975 also seems of small consequence to Titov and his supporters.

Titov was lucky to have ousted Gander in time for the Moscow Olympics. For him to turn around and encourage those same countries that voted him into office to name an American to the Technical Committee would negate the gains the Soviets had made. Frank Cumiskey, a three-time Olympian from Union City, New Jersey, did have his name placed in nomination in 1976. But he and a Canadian split the Western votes and Urvary of Hungary got in instead. That was quite a coup for the USSR, trading what could have been years of headaches with Gander and Cumiskey for the solace of Titov and Urvary. By the way, the tally in the Titov vs. Gander balloting was 27 to 25—the barest majority considering that fifty-two nations voted—and Titov was more than lucky to win. The Russians reportedly footed the bill for several South American delegates to come to Montreal and vote against Gander.

Without his chairmanship of the Technical Committee to fall back on, Gander was by these measures summarily removed from the international gymnastics scene. He is now retired and lives in Chiasso, Switzerland, a little town on the Swiss-Italian border thirty kilometers from Milan. He has been invited to come to the United States on several occasions, but has thus far declined. Most evenings he just relaxes and enjoys a good bottle of wine. So it goes.

The fact that some of the rulemakers are sometimes rulebreakers is not the worst facet of the Technical Committee's operation. The sport could probably weather the damage done by a few villains—even those in high places. What's worse is the standard of behavior these people set for—and eventually impose upon—the rest of the member nations. First, they ignore the rules enough themselves to create a climate in which everybody thinks he has to cheat in order to keep pace. Then, when most everybody *does* cheat, the whole thing can be dismissed as a harmless boys-will-be-boys kind of thing. And nothing much can be done to change the existing order because at this point there aren't enough straight people left to get upset about it. As far as certification of judges is concerned, the

When the scores from his jury do not conform to certain criteria, a superior judge must call a conference and ask at least one of the four to reconsider his mark.

TC will accept any man nominated by the gymnastics federation of his country and will assign him to international meets, just as long as he has passed the necessary judges' course. It doesn't matter if he isn't the most qualified man available at the time (the better to control him later?), if he is extremely biased (perhaps he will hate the Americans and Japanese!), or even if he happens to be a coach of his national team (the more willing he'll be to arrange tradeoffs).

How can a judge also be a coach of his national team? Easy. It doesn't matter whose name is listed as coach in the program, who wears the dirty sweatshirt in practice, or who spends the nights of competition spotting guys on the high bar. The coach is the man who is in charge back home. And many international judges are, even though they try to hide the fact during meets. But if you see one hanging around his national team's workouts all week, chances are pretty good that he is a coach. Obviously, this makes any pretense of objectivity a sham. It also brings up a very good question: If there is a Code of Points for gymnasts, why isn't there a Code of Ethics for judges?

Even if there were, it wouldn't stop the Technical Committee from affecting the outcome of every big international meet. By virtue of their positions, each of the six regular members gets to serve as superior judge on an event at the Olympics or World Championships, while the chairman acts as director of the meet. A superior judge has almost limitless powers and, according to the worth of the man, this can be good or bad. His most basic task is supervising the work of the four judges (called the jury, for ominous reasons) who serve under him. He also scores every competitor, but his mark doesn't ordinarily count. Instead, he collects four little slips of paper from the jury, throws out the high and low marks, and averages the middle two, thereby arriving at a preliminary score for each exercise. However, the crowd doesn't get to see it yet. If the score is 9.6 or higher, the superior judge must check to see that the middle scores are no more than

.1 apart—or "within range." If they are, the preliminary score becomes the final score. If they aren't within range, the superior judge must call a conference and convince one of the jury members to reconsider his first mark. If the preliminary score is between 9.0 and 9.55, the middle scores must not vary by more than .2, and so on. There's more. If the high and low scores are too far out of line with his overall impression of the exercise, the superior judge may ask that they be changed, too. In fact, a superior judge may call a conference *whenever* he feels something is amiss—even when the scores are in keeping with the rules. (This must have been the case when Gonzalez questioned Azarian's wisdom in Montreal, because when all was said and done, no scores were changed.) A superior judge even has carte blanche to add his own score to the pot if he is displeased with the decision of the jury. To do so, he averages the middle scores, adds his own score, and divides by two, thus arriving at a final mark which is 50 percent his own.

About the only privilege denied a superior judge is the right to interfere in another superior judge's event, which is solely the duty of the TC chairman. That's why it should have been Lylo, not Shakhlin, who intervened in the Gonzalez-Azarian dispute. By the same token, it should have been Lylo, not Gander, who got Shakhlin back in line. But given the dire nature of the situation and the latitude that superior judges enjoy, is it any wonder that Shakhlin saw no embarrassment in leaving the high bar and walking all the way across the arena to argue for his country's cause? Nor was it his last attempt at sabotage.

After four events, Japan had pulled ahead by .2 of a point. The Soviets cut the margin to .1 after five, and as the final events of the team competition got underway, Shakhlin was no doubt convinced that he could still pull out the gold medal for Mother Russia. He and Titov and Azarian had been teammates on the last Soviet Olympic team to defeat the Japanese in 1956. Now, twenty years later, they would have their revenge.

145

145

After all, how could .1 hold up when Shakhlin had the Japanese right where he wanted them—on high bar. With the Soviet men right next door on floor exercise, he could monitor their scores at the same time. Unfortunately for Shakhlin, the Japanese were all planning to go for broke. So the four scores for each man were likely to be too close to tamper with—either feast or famine.

The first man up, Hiroshi Kajiyama, did very little that anyone could call into question. Shakhlin looked at the scores from his jury and frowned: 9.8, 9.8, 9.7, and 9.7. Reluctantly, he allowed a 9.75 to be flashed to the crowd. Hisato Igarishi executed a perfect pike-to-layout, double back dismount and again the scores were within range: 9.9, 9.8, 9.9, and 9.7. Shakhlin had to try something. He couldn't afford to let a 9.85 stand when he had just seen the first Russian score on floor—only 9.55! He called the high bar judges into conference, hoping to get one of the 9.9s reduced to a 9.8, which would have reduced Igarishi's final score to 9.8. But as Shakhlin was making his pitch, officials from the U.S., French, and Japanese delegations began exhorting the crowd to make some noise and let Shakhlin know he was being watched. After five minutes of futility, Shakhlin gave up and allowed the 9.85 to be posted. He was of no further trouble to the Japanese. Kato threw in a solid 9.75, Eizo Kenmotsu hit perhaps the best routine of his life for another 9.85, and Tsukahara's 9.9 brought the house down.

Considering the inane manner in which the sport has been run for nearly a century (the FIG was founded in 1881), gymnastics deserves most of the political problems. it has encountered. When a sport which dates back to ancient Greece and which has been part of the modern Olympic Games since their revival in 1896, goes without a rulebook until 1964—that's 1964 *anno Domini*—it is asking for High Anxiety. Furthermore, when a sport which depends upon subjective analysis for the awarding of medals engages in international competition for sixty-eight years with no formal guidelines as to how that analysis is to be performed, it begins to look foolish from within as well as from without. And when members lose respect for the organization they belong to and, in the absence of any penalties, decide that anything goes, they create the abuse-of-power situation that ensnares the FIG today.

For most of those sixty-eight years, a judge's only reference points as far as scoring went were his own experiences as a gymnast. That led to several thousand differences of opinion right there. If a gymnast was lucky, he got a judge who critiqued his routine against the other competitors. Lucky, that is, unless he happened to be first up. More often than not, judges relied on what was called "general impression."

Arthur Gander was the first to get really fed up. After his Swiss team was beaten out by the Finns amid some highly questionable scoring at the London Games in 1948 (he was the delegation chief of Switzerland in those days), Gander began looking for a standardized, objective way to measure exercises. His first attempt at a rulebook was a twelve-page booklet written in French and German which amounted to little more than a few sheets of paper stapled together. It did contain the notion that judges should break an exercise down into three parts—difficulty, execution, and combination—but nobody paid much attention. General impression was a lot simpler, although the results tended to vary with what side of the bed the judge got up on. Gander helped produce a more sophisticated version in 1956, the year he became chairman of the TC. But the first real *Code de pointage* did not appear until 1964. By the summer of 1968—after gymnastics had been through sixteen Olympic Games and sixteen World Championships—the *Code* was even translated into English.

Despite the ongoing war of words between East and West, the overall quality of international judging has improved immeasurably since 1948. Clinics have helped, such as the one Gander chaired in Rome in

1968. It lasted five days and after forty hours of lectures, the judges had to submit to a five-hour written exam. Only those who passed were certified for the 1968 Olympics in Mexico City. Under Gander's stewardship, the clinic idea caught on and it is now customary for judges, like gymnasts, to have to qualify for the Olympics. An oath of honesty must also be taken at a meeting just before the start of the Games; unfortunately, no one checks to see which judges have their fingers crossed behind their backs.

Tom Maloney, a former coach at West Point, remembers the first time he ever judged an international meet. "God, was I impressed! I heard nothing but lofty thoughts before the start of the competition. And when the judges joined hands to take the oath, I got kind of choked up. Then the meet began, and they all threw the rulebook out the window."

Back in Montreal at a meeting before the start of the 1976 team competition, Karl Heinz Zschocke of East Germany, the TC member who was to be superior judge on floor exercise, made an impassioned plea for a strict adherence to the Code of Points. To the members of his floor-ex jury, Zschocke was particularly adamant. "I mean that if a man does not hold his strength move for two seconds, you *must* take .2 off!" Zschocke orchestrated the sentence with several sweeping movements of his arms, and from the tone of his voice it sounded as though he meant the rule to apply even to a judge's mother. But after the joining of hands and the oath-taking came the throwing-the-rulebook-out-the-window part. When the Russians rotated to floor-ex, Nikolai Andrianov, the eventual All-Around champion, did just what Zschocke had warned his jury about—only worse. He didn't hold his strength part *at all*. Andrianov pressed up to a handstand, but passed right through it and went immediately to his next move. The penalty for making this kind of mistake during the compulsory portion of the team championships should be considerable. Forget the .2 deduction for not holding *long enough*; according to the rules,

Andrianov should have been docked .5. (On parallel bars the same mistake can cost you a whole point.) When Andrianov didn't show a hold part anywhere else in his routine and looked rather ragged in spots, there was discussion among opposing coaches that he would be lucky to make 9.0. Zschocke's men didn't see it that way, however. Without undue hesitation, the judges awarded Andrianov a 9.45. No conference was called.

It is hard to believe the superior judge could have missed what was going on, but easy to believe he would have dismissed it. Such things happen in Europe all the time. Or Zschocke, like Shakhlin and some of his other colleagues on the Technical Committee, might have had his mind on some other event. For example, as the team competition was winding to a close the next night and the main plot involving the Japanese and the Russians was being played out, Zschocke's East German team was trying to hold onto third place against a furious charge by Hungary. So as the last events got underway and Zschocke was allegedly giving his full attention to the Russians on floor exercise, he was also keeping tabs on the bronze-medal fight going on at the pommel horse and rings. Parallel bar competition was finished and without a team to worry about, Jalantie of Finland could relax. But Mercia Badulescu, a Romanian who was judging parallel bars, was keeping an eye on Kaneko at the vault to see how he was treating the Romanians, who, in turn, were trying to pull out fifth place from the West Germans. They failed by .1 and no doubt attributed part of the blame to Kaneko, who was stealing glances at Shakhlin and the Japanese team on high bar. It was like Oscar night in Hollywood—you needed a half-dozen remote cameras just to keep up with what the losers were doing.

The longer you play the International Gymnastics game, the more likely you are to feel that world politics is the root of all evil. But it is only one of the Seven Deadly Virtues of International Judging. It is by

far the worst, but there are still six more.

The Honest Mistake: In matters of taste, you never have complete agreement. While one judge might see a bend in the knees on pommel horse as a slight break and deduct .1, a second judge looking at the same move from a slightly different angle might consider it a major faux pas and take off .3. As is written in the Code of Points: "It is not only a purely mathematical or theoretical problem to. define, estimate, and classify value parts, but the judge must also possess the ability to perform in his mind the exercise to be judged. Continuous observation of the trends and development in artistic gymnastics, nationally and internationally, and unrestricted knowledge of the rules and regulations are necessary for conscientious judging." Other than that, there's nothing to it.

Ignorance Is Bliss: By using a unique system of shorthand and keeping their eyes on their own business, a lot of judges actually try to uphold the Code of Points. Others are intimidated by 212 pages of rules. They take the easy way out and just flash a score. General Impression rides again.

The Star System: Certain judges might ignore the omission of a hold part—but only for a champion like Andrianov whose reputation precedes him to the mat. If somebody else leaves it out, the judges leave .5 out of his score. The "up to's" are handled in the same way. The Code of Points stipulates that a judge may deduct "up to .3" for a bend in the knees on pommel horse. This gives the judge some leeway to distinguish between major and minor breaks in form. But when a star is involved, the "up to" serves a different purpose. If Andrianov bends his knees on pommel horse, most judges say to themselves, "Andrianov is a great, great gymnast and I don't want to be the one to underscore him. That knee bend was such a tiny flaw in an otherwise wonderful routine, I think I'll only take .1 off." When a run-of-the-mill gymnast bends his knees the same way, he loses .3 every time. Incidentally, a popular offshoot of the Star System is the Famous

Team Syndrome.

The Staircase Effect: To avoid what happened on the women's side in Montreal, where judges started off giving 9.8s and then had to award 10.0s to show their appreciation for something better, men's judges will purposely hold down the scores of the first few competitors up on an event. It's a question of philosophical pride and sheer mathematics. After you've told somebody that he's "perfect," where do you go from there? You can't give him an 11.0.

Fear of Crowds: Despite the cavalier manner in which some judges show their disregard for the rules, nobody likes to be put on the spot by a roaring mob. If it's merely an Honest Mistake, a huge crowd demonstration might cause a judge to reconsider his mark and give the gymnast the benefit of the doubt. If it's a World Politics situation, the judge in question has to be careful; he doesn't want to get a reputation for this sort of thing. The Cerar-Shakhlin demonstration in Prague marked the first time in the history of the World Championships that foot-stomping decided who would win a gold medal. But the most talked-about spectator rebellion in gymnastics history remains the Doris Fuchs incident which took place at the 1966 World Championships in Dortmund, West Germany. Fuchs was a member of the U.S. women's team, but she had been born in Germany. She did a superb routine on the uneven bars and the judges gave her a reasonably good mark, although not nearly as good as the crowd thought she deserved. When a change in score wasn't forthcoming, they went berserk—for over an hour. An East German woman tried four different times to start her floor-ex routine, but had to stop because she couldn't hear her music. This was back in the days of open scoring for men and women, when judges had to hold up their marks so the people in the audience could see them. By the end of the evening, every judge on the floor was somebody's favorite villain. Open scoring was done away with after the 1968 Olympics, although for a slightly different reason.

Gander could sympathize with Eastern European judges who were under extreme pressure to deliver big scores for athletes from their area of the globe. He theorized that the problem could be eased somewhat if a judge didn't have to make his scores public. Gander's supporters say it was the only mistake he ever made. It was a big one. Closed scoring took the meet away from the fans and put it in the hands of the superior judges. Their story has already been told, and the web of secrecy surrounding a judge's ballot has made it even more difficult to bring pressure against those who deliver big scores on demand. Think of it this way, a man like Albert Azarian is oblivious to most means of intimidation. Yet not even Azarian would have the audacity to hold up a piece of cardboard with 10.0 written on it time after time.

$1 + 1 = 3$: In this era of electronic scoreboards, pocket calculators, and uneasy coaches, tampering with the official math would seem to be the most difficult way to fudge the outcome of a meet. That hasn't stopped some people from trying. In April 1977, Kurt Thomas was asked to compete in the Romanian Invitational. When he arrived in Europe he thought he knew why. Romanian Danut Grecu, a nationwide hero, had won the meet several years running. Thomas had apparently been imported to serve as a sacrificial lamb. But after a real tug-of-war with the judges, Thomas managed to eke out a 55.55 to 55.35 win over Grecu in the All-Around. The Romanian team and coaches were so astonished by the final tally that they swarmed over the scorer's table to protest. When the official results were released two days later, Thomas was still the winner, but his margin had shrunk to .1. In the floor exercise finals, Kurt came in tied with Ion Checiches of Romania, both gymnasts having scored 9.4 in the preliminaries. When Thomas scored 9.4 and saw Checiches' 9.3 flashed to the crowd, he knew he had won the event. Except when it came time for the awards ceremony, Checiches was announced as co-champion. An interpreter said the

original score had been protested on the spot and raised a tenth. The meet directors insisted that Thomas defend his title at the 1978 Romanian Invitational. Apparently Grecu was looking for revenge. Thomas won again, but it took a miracle. His final margin this time was .05, and he was so consistently underscored that in four of the six events a protest was lodged in his behalf. A check of the "official" scoresheets the judges have to sign after each rotation revealed twelve discrepancies between them and the slips of paper the superior judges had been collecting for three days.

If this "scandal of international judging" were in the least bit subtle, it might lend an element of excitement to the sport. Everybody likes a good spy novel, and this kind of intrigue might even sell tickets. But in place of dark, sinister forces, gymnastics is overrun with conspicuous cheaters and unbridled chauvinists—the kind of overly anxious subversives who warrant calling in Inspector Clouseau, not Scotland Yard.

There is no improving the situation as long as East-West political relations remain as they are. The Russians aren't likely to change, that's for sure. Soviet ice skating judges became so notorious for their biases that in 1977 the International Skating Union banned them from the World European Championships. It has been suggested that neutral judging—no one being in a position to judge an athlete from his home country—will help solve the problem. Nope. Tradeoffs are just as effective as getting to judge your own countrymen, and besides, underscoring the enemy accomplishes the same purpose. Instant replay machines were used for the first time at the 1976 Olympics and were supposed to revolutionize judging. But given the personalities involved, they tend to start as many arguments as they settle. Perhaps Tom Zivic's "Why fight it?" philosophy makes the most sense. Because when you try to attack the problem with reason, it only leads to frustration.

The following interview took place in New York in March 1979 during workouts before the Dial-American

Cup at Madison Square Garden. The principals, who communicated with each other through an interpreter, were an American journalist and Vladimir Makarin, a Russian gymnastics coach.

Reporter: Are you familiar with the incident at the Montreal Olympics when Boris Shakhlin left his position at the high bar to argue with the rings judge over a Japanese score?

Makarin: Yes. No family is without its beasts.

Reporter: Is this the way you think international judging should be, with political considerations weighing as heavily as they do?

Makarin: A judge should look only at the work. Nothing else.

Reporter: What do you think of judging in your part of the world?

Makarin: It is honest and very fair.

Reporter: And you do disagree with what Shakhlin did, causing Gander, the president of the FIG, to intercede?

Makarin: He should never have left his position. He should never wield his power in that fashion. He was the one who was at fault.

Reporter (sensing a scoop): Shakhlin was at fault, right?

Makarin: Nyet. *Gander.*

A gymnast performing outdoors on the rings around the turn of the century.

History

The incident happened soon enough after the massacre of Israeli athletes in Munich that when people first got a glimpse of his face peeking out from behind the bleachers, many of them feared he was another terrorist. His features were distorted by a pantyhose mask and when he walked out onto the floor just before the start of the 1974 NCAA meet, a lot of people in the stands couldn't see what else he was wearing. That was just it—he wasn't wearing anything else.

The dude was *nude*. Bare-ass naked from the neck down. At first the crowd gasped in alarm. Then, when they realized what the man was up to, they roared loud enough to blow the roof off old Recreation Hall at Penn State University. It took him maybe five seconds to reach the floor exercise mat, where he paused long enough to let the judges know he was about to start his routine. And he was. With form that left nothing to the imagination, he went out and did a roundoff, followed by a back handspring and a back somersault. He stuck his landing, paused to acknowledge the cheering, then bolted out the doors at the end of the arena with a campus policeman in hot pursuit.

Despite the pantyhose mask, there were indications that the man was a redhead. But Penn State coach Gene Wettstone didn't need any clues; the act spoke for itself. He was positive it was Jim Culhane. And if he knew Culhane, which Wettstone did, having coached him at Penn State during the mid-1960s, the police were in for a rough time. Sure enough, even though the temperature outside on that evening in April of 1974 wasn't too far above freezing, Culhane led the campus cop on a merry chase. After perhaps a quarter mile, he was able to double back around and hop into a VW van that he had stationed in the Rec Hall parking lot. Within five minutes, he was dressed and back in his seat for the start of the competition. The only thing he missed were his marks. The routine itself was worth at least 9.6, and even though Wettstone was a bit perturbed that the tranquility of his opening ceremonies had been shattered, he allowed that with the risk and originality factors involved, Culhane probably deserved a score of 10.0.

Undoubtedly, some of the people who witnessed Culhane's brief, but spectacular appearance at the 1974 NCAAs thought he was an international gymnastics scandal all by himself. Had they known the full extent of his flakiness, they would have been sure of it. But in his own special way, James Patrick Culhane, Jr., of Rochester, New York, was paying tribute to his immediate, not-so-recent, and ancient ancestors in gymnastics—to those crazies of the 1960s who became trapeze artists, movie stuntmen, and circus clowns; to one of the sport's founding fathers, Friedrich Jahn, who was not only pursued by police but even imprisoned for his support of gymnastics; and to the very first gymnasts of ancient Greece who were taught by Plato and Aristotle and who also performed their back flips in the nude.

That shouldn't come as much of a surprise, because the word *gymnastics* is derived from the Greek *gymnós*, meaning "naked." *Gymnastics* literally means "naked exercise." Or, if you prefer, "strip and go tumble." At any rate, this etymological explanation should make it clear that Culhane did not "streak the NCAAs," as the story is so often told. He was merely reenacting the ancient Olympic custom of removing the loin cloth, a practice begun for aesthetic reasons in 720 B.C., which may also account for why the women of Greece were forbidden to watch the Games.

At the height of the classical period in Greece, during the fifth and fourth centuries B.C., a young man's body was expected to be as pure and properly developed as his mind. In fact, physical training was a requirement for citizenship. At this point in history, *gymnastics* did not stand for the specific set of disciplines at which Kurt Thomas excels. Rather it was a catch-all term for a variety of athletic events which made up the earliest Olympic programs: running, jumping, lifting and throwing weights, wrestling, and one more which is

Gymnasts depicted on an ancient
Greek vase

the foundation of modern gymnastics—tumbling.

The athletes of Greece honed their skills at training centers known as *gymnasiums,* or "schools for naked exercise." Membership was usually restricted to males over the age of eighteen, and every major city in the country had at least one gymnasium. The facilities consisted of vast areas for competition and bathing, but there were also great hallways adorned with paintings and statues and even lecture halls where literature and philosophy were discussed. Athens had three gymnasiums: the Cynosargus; the Academia, where Plato taught; and the Lyceum, where Aristotle taught.

When Greek civilization declined 150 years before Christ, the Romans adopted the idea of gymnasiums. But in A.D. 392, Emperor Theodosius I put an end to compulsory physical training and decreed that the Olympic Games be abolished after more than 1,100 years. Theodosius was to be the last emperor of the united Roman Empire and he had more important uses for the athletes of the day; he needed all the able-bodied men he could find to send into battle in Gaul and Italy.

The Romans did retain one vestige of Greek sporting society because of its military value: the wooden horse. Not the large, mythological variety that foiled the Trojans, but a small, equestrian device used to teach Greek youths how to mount and dismount. It even had a real horse's tail affixed to one end and a raised neck on the other. Though the apparatus was never part of the ancient Olympic Games, its practical use as a riding tool accounts for why it was faithfully passed on from generation to generation and civilization to civilization until in nineteenth-century Europe someone finally thought to replace the saddle with two pommels and build a gymnastic exercise around it.

The wooden horse dates back much further than Greco-Roman times, to man's earliest attempts to domesticate the horse in Asia around 3000 B.C. And in Minoan Crete, 1,300 years before the Olympics, a similar device was probably used in connection with a bizarre ritual called bull-leaping. This rodeo-like event began with a brave member of the community clinging to the back of a stampeding bull. The rider would then grab one of the animal's horns, swing around in front of the bull's head, and land back on the neck or rump. At least that was the plan. To maximize his chances of survival, the rider must have practiced on a makeshift bull made out of wood and covered with leather. Add a swiveling head topped by a pair of hornlike pommels and you have yet another forerunner of the side horse.

With the disintegration of the West Roman Empire in the fourth and fifth centuries, physical exercise fell into almost total neglect. From the Middle Ages to the Renaissance, the only organized physical activity of any significance involved knights—and jousting was more violent than athletic. However, among the medieval legends there is a story of a German knight renowned for his ability to leap over six horses while in full armor. Besides being a bit superhuman, this knight must have required at least six wooden horses to practice with, and thus, the long horse vault was discovered.

As for its cousin, the side horse, by the 1700s the French had named it *voltiger,* because you had to "flutter" over the apparatus like a butterfly. However, they weren't using it in the gymnasium, but in the recital halls of the finest finishing schools as a device for teaching rich, young gentlemen how to move about Parisian society in an elegant manner. After all, if monsieur could master a set of leg scissors on the horse, then learning the minuet would be child's play. And if he could keep his toes pointed on a series of leg circles, he would have no trouble with that dramatic stretch of the instep when he bowed to a mademoiselle on the ballroom floor. The Germans have always found the French somewhat effeminate, at least in comparison to themselves. So when they discovered that their name for the horse meant "to flutter," the Germans changed it to *schwingel* or "swinger"—which

they felt was infinitely better.

A new wave of classicism was spreading through Germany in the eighteenth and nineteenth centuries, bringing with it not only a revival of interest in art, literature, and philosophy, but also greater devotion to one's physical well being. At the same time, a shift in power was taking place all over the continent of Europe. The man behind it was Napoleon Bonaparte, and when he marched triumphantly into Berlin in 1806, his French forces having occupied all of what is now Germany, the resultant clash of cultures made for instant rebellion among those being occupied. Not from very many of the occupied, because most of the German aristocracy were conspiring with Napoleon. But one of the most influential leaders in the people's revolt against the French was a man named Friedrich Ludwig Jahn.

Jahn was a high school teacher who established a gymnastics club called a *turnverein* outside Berlin in 1811. It was located at the Hasenheide, an open-air gymnasium which still serves as a public meeting place today. At first, Jahn's pupils came solely for gymnastics instruction. The facilities included scaffolds from which rings and ladders were suspended, climbing poles and ladders, pits for broad jumping and high jumping, and also a side horse. But in addition Jahn gave them a piece of his mind. He preached that the French way of living, emulated all over Europe, was making the Germans too soft. Jahn was able to get away with saying such things because, to the French, he always sounded like he was talking about muscles, not politics. Nevertheless, Jahn's turnverein quickly became a center for German nationalism and for talk of the eventual overthrow of Napoleon, which was not long in coming.

In 1812, while Napoleon and his forces were away suffering a devastating defeat in Russia and anti-French sentiment was growing stronger in and around Berlin, Jahn and his aides were looking for new movements and apparatus to stimulate his pupils' interest in gymnastics. He had been teaching them to use a beam not unlike the modern balance beam that women gymnasts use. But Jahn decided this needed steam-lining. What he came up with was a thin horizontal bar similar to that which the Flemish master Pieter Brueghel depicted in his famous watercolor entitled, "Children's Games." Jahn's new device was almost exactly like the present-day high bar. In an effort to help his students strengthen their arms and shoulders for side horse work, Jahn set about redesigning the climbing bars. Until now, they had been used mainly for walking hand-over-hand in monkey fashion. But with the rungs removed, a person could swing freely between the long supporting poles and even pull himself up into what today we would call an L-support. Jahn christened his new invention the *barren*, which we know as the parallel bars.

Napoleon's soldiers were so impressed with Jahn's new apparatus that during the War of Liberation they often stole them and used them for firewood. Jahn was away at the time serving in the Prussian army. When the French were driven from Germany in 1815, he returned to Berlin. His interest in his new inventions had not waned, but he was distracted by the continuing fight for liberalism with the reigning monarch, who was now a Prussian but no less a problem than Napoleon. Thus, Jahn left most of the parallel bar instruction up to a young man named Friesen.

It is important to reiterate that in the context of nineteenth-century Germany, gymnastics was not merely a sport. Jahn's doctrine of physical and intellectual freedom had galvanized anti-French sentiment into a political movement. But if anything, repression was even more severe under King Frederick William III. That, plus some wanton violence, transformed Jahn's teachings into something of a religion. Friesen, the parallel bars instructor, got into an argument over which mode of thought was right and was beaten to death. The other side had its losses, too. A German poet made some nasty remarks about gymnastics and

A forerunner of the high bar appears in this small segment of "Children's Games," painted by Pieter Bruegel the Elder in 1560.

all who took part in it. He was murdered.

By 1819, the Turners, as Jahn's followers were now called, had become too large and too vocal a minority for the king to ignore. Hoping to destroy their movement, he sent Jahn to prison and closed his turnverein at the Hasenheide.

The Turners went underground. They met secretly in barns, dancehalls, and factories at odd hours of the day and night, wherever and whenever they could get together for talk and exercise without being harassed. These circumstances dictated a change in apparatus, from the cumbersome outdoor equipment designed to withstand the elements to more portable models which could be carted around from place to place—sometimes on the run. The shape of the side horse had to be simplified. The neck and croup were eliminated so that both ends were flat. The saddle portion was replaced by two pommels five to six inches high so that a person could get a better grip on the apparatus both during competition and between hurried trips from the barn to the factory. The parallel bars were made adjustable, which was an important development for two reasons. When both bars were raised, a man could hang from his upper arms and do a variety of new tricks not possible when the bars were stationed close to the ground. And when women found parallel bar work too taxing for their particular physical makeup, one of the bars was lowered to approximate today's uneven bars.

Friedrich Jahn's contributions to history did not end with his term in prison, which lasted six years. He was still one of the most revered and active men in Germany at the age of seventy, and his name can be found in any book of reference. Invariably his biographical sketch begins: Jahn, Friedrich Ludwig (1778–1852), German patriot *and gymnast.*

By the 1860s, Jahn's theories on gymnastics were being challenged by the followers of Pehr Henrik Ling (1776–1839), a Swedish educator who had something different in mind. While Jahn had envisioned gymnastics to be a competitive struggle of Man vs. Ap-

paratus with endless possibilities for achievement and invention, Ling saw it as pure physical education for the masses. Sometimes *en masse.* It was not unheard of for 10,000 of Ling's disciples to congregate in one place to perform a series of movements in unison. In order to keep everything synchronized, a leader would give verbal commands to which the group would respond, rather like robots. Ling felt that through mass exercise without apparatus people would disregard their competitive urges and concentrate on achieving a oneness of artistic form. The result was truly kaleidoscopic when viewed from above: 10,000 deep knee bends, 10,000 cartwheels, 10,000 headstands. It isn't clear whether Ling wanted to control his subject's minds as well as their bodies (there was something Nazi-like about those group demonstrations), or whether he merely sought to provide them with a more active form of yoga. He claimed only to be interested in building up weak bodies. The two systems were such opposites that no one could have foreseen they would one day be aligned. But in the 1920s, the Federation Internationale de Gymnastique finally stepped in and resolved the sixty-year feud.

In its most innocent stages the Ling-Jahn fight had consisted mainly of petty name-calling. At one point the Ling people charged that Jahn's movements were violent in appearance and potentially dangerous to the gymnast, and they singled out the parallel bars for their severest criticism: "Not only do they endanger the health, they degrade the human body to the level of a mechanical pendulum." But when three different team gold medals had to be awarded at the 1912 Olympics because no one had determined which movements should be performed in a standard Olympic program, the FIG had to do something. What they came up with was a format based on the philosophies of both Ling and Jahn. Ling's attention to perfect form and rhythm became the basis for the compulsory exercises, wherein a gymnast is asked to perform relatively simple maneuvers, but is judged according

Gene Wettstone, coach at Penn
State from 1938 to 1976, produced twenty-five NCAA champions and ten Olympians.

Swedish national team performing
synchronized calisthenics at Penn
State in 1954.

to how precisely he executes them. Jahn was the Thomas Edison of gymnastics and he saw the apparatus as adding to the difficulty, art, and excitement of the sport. Thus, his free-style movements formed the basis for the optional exercises.

It was in this manner that Ling and Jahn, a real Yin and Yang combination if there ever was one, became the parents of modern gymnastics.

When Europeans began emigrating to the United States in great numbers during the 1800s, gymnastics was one of the old world customs they threw in the trunk to take with them. Thus, Turner history and U.S. gymnastics history are intertwined. Looking back, the most revered American coach of them all was Wettstone of Penn State, who learned his gymnastics at a turnverein in his hometown of Union City, New Jersey; the finest judge and technical expert was Frank Cumiskey, a boyhood friend of Wettstone's and another Union City Turner; the administrative genius who brought U.S. gymnastics out of the Dark Ages, Frank Bare, was originally a member of a St. Louis turnverein before he became executive director of the United States Gymnastics Federation; Bill Roetzheim, who was elected president of the USGF in 1978, was a Chicago Turner; and ten of the first twelve Olympic gymnastics teams were coached by men who belonged to turnvereins from California to New York.

But when the Olympic Games reconvened in Athens on April 6, 1896, after a gap of 1,504 years, the United States gymnastics team was not there. Neither were a lot of others. The problem was that in those days you couldn't just hop on a dinner flight at Kennedy Airport and wake up in Greece the next morning. You had to go by boat, and by the time you arrived you might be too old to compete. Consequently, most countries didn't engage in international gymnastics competition unless it came to them. Only five teams competed in Athens, and while a group of old world Turners was helping Germany win most of the gold medals, their counterparts in America were concentrating on the National AAUs, an annual event sponsored by the Amateur Athletic Union which would not yield center stage to the Olympics until 1920.

The Paris Games of 1900 showed the Americans they weren't missing much. Scheduled in conjunction with the World Exposition, or World's Fair as it came to be known, the athletic competition lasted for five months and came off looking like a sideshow. In the end, the gymnastics All-Around was won by a Frenchman, Gustave Sandras, who had to be a combination of Bruce Jenner and Kurt Thomas to do it. It seems that the 1900 All-Around competition consisted of the six modern-day gymnastic events, plus rope climbing, high jumping, pole vaulting, and throwing a 110-pound weight—which is about all some of today's gymnasts weigh.

St. Louis hosted the 1904 Olympics and, according to the record books, the U.S. gymnastics team was unbeatable, winning nearly every event. What the stats don't tell you is that the Games were again tacked onto the World's Fair and that 107 of the 119 gymnasts who competed were Americans. That made winning pretty easy. In fact, the whole thing was such a farce as an Olympics that it was allowed to count as that year's National AAU meet.

To make up for Paris and St. Louis, the Games were held in a modest way two years later in Athens. Again the United States sent no gymnastics team. The London Games of 1908 helped establish the Olympics as a world-wide athletic spectacle. Albert Braglia of Italy won the first of two consecutive All-Around titles and Sweden won the team gymnastics championship. The 1912 Stockholm Olympics belonged to Jim Thorpe, the American track and field star who finished either first or second in every event of the decathlon and pentathlon, and whose heroics helped to obscure the confusion which reigned in the gymnastics competition. Because the FIG had not yet settled on the compulsory-optional framework or on the exact nature of the exercises to be done in each phase, the 1912 team champion was Sweden. And Norway. And Italy. The Swedes won a gold medal for their group performances in the Ling style, the Norwegians won a gold for "free choice of movements and apparatus," and the Italians were awarded a gold "according to special conditions" —which these certainly were.

World War I canceled the 1916 Games, and no Central European nations had recovered sufficiently to compete in 1920. The Soviet Union could have but decided not to, which was only fitting since it meant that the Russians and the Americans were going in opposite directions right from the start. While the United States was sending its first Olympic gymnastics team to Antwerp in 1920, the USSR was disappearing from the international scene until 1952. It wasn't that the Russians didn't like to compete or weren't interested in keeping fit, they just didn't think the "bourgeois" nations of the world were fit to compete against.

In post-Revolutionary Russia, gymnastics again became a political football just as it had in Germany. Its devotees extolled the wonders it did for the body; its opponents decried its lack of teamwork. This controversy was not to be taken lightly, because gymnastics had always occupied an extremely important niche in the Russian way of life.

When the Russian Gymnastics Society was created in 1883 (the first national federation of any Russian sport), Anton Chekhov expressed the hope that the society's members were "the people of the future. The time will come when everyone will be as strong and fit: There lie the nation's hopes and happiness." Even Lenin was a believer. While locked up in a St. Petersburg prison for some early political activities, Lenin wrote letters to friends saying he was able to pass the time by doing "gymnastics with great pleasure and value *every day*." The italics were Lenin's, and after the workers' revolution of 1917, he often stressed the role of gymnastics in the new socialistic state. "Young

people," he wrote, "need a zest for living; healthy sport—gymnastics, swimming, hiking, all manner of physical exercise—should be combined as much as possible with a variety of intellectual interests that will give young people healthy minds in healthy bodies."

In the immediate post-Revolutionary period, gymnastics started out to be just what it had been in ancient Greece: an Rx for living. In 1921, the Soviet Commissar of Enlightenment invited Isadora Duncan to Moscow and helped her set up an academy. She taught there for two years, long enough to influence not only Soviet modern dance but artistic gymnastics as well.

However, a great controversy between rival factions was brewing. This time it had nothing to do with gymnastic movements, as it had in Germany, but with the fact that the sport was associated with foreign systems. Or, as the Proletkultists put it, "All organized sports that emanate from bourgeois society are remnants of the decadent past and reflections of degenerate bourgeois culture." The Hygienists argued that it ran contrary to the Socialist ethic for Russia to engage in any kind of athletic competition which had nationalistic overtones and which glorified the contributions of the individual, and they swung enough weight to get gymnastics excluded from the first Trade Union Games of 1925. It was also barred from Soviet schools, but within a decade had made a complete comeback.

By the time World War II ended, the Soviets were anxious to render all previous statements concerning the evils of athletic competition against other nations inoperative. There was political hay to be made by beating your enemies in athletics. Although very few Russian athletes (other than chess grandmasters) had competed internationally since 1916, most of the Soviet sports organizations had been able to produce athletes of world-class caliber through intranational games. The Red Sports Gymnastics Organization felt its men had been ready to tackle the world since 1941, and by the time the 1952 Olympics rolled around, Russian gym-

H. G. Newhart of the Naval Academy, one of the first U.S. All-Arounders, 1927.

nasts had quietly become the best in the world.

Even though the Soviets hadn't been competing internationally, their coaches had been watching what was going on. This put them in the unique position of knowing how strong the opposition was without revealing anything about their own progress. Sensing that one big Olympics could equal the work of a hundred foreign ambassadors, the Russians rejoined all the important international sports federations (the FIG in 1948) and chose the 1952 Games in nearby Helsinki as the time and place for their long-anticipated return. They were the primary attraction, winning sixty-nine total medals, good for second place behind the U.S. But nowhere were they more impressive than in gymnastics. "Oh my God, look at that!" was all anybody could say as Viktor Chukarin and his teammates unveiled a whole new set of strength moves on the rings. The Russians were not only stronger than anyone else, they were also daring, innovative, and absolutely sure of themselves. They ran away with the team championship, Chukarin won the All-Around, and he was joined by four teammates in the top seven.

Judging from their margin of victory over the Swiss and defending-champion Finns, the Russians seemed on the verge of a dynasty. But hidden amid all the statistics from Helsinki was an omen of things to come: The Japanese had managed to finish fifth with only a five-man team. Since all the other powers competed with eight and counted only their best five scores on each event, this was quite an achievement. What's more, on two events, floor exercise and vault, the Japanese five had outscored the Russians.

Compared to the Soviets, who had stood in the wings for years rehearsing and looking for just the right moment to make their debut, the Japanese were a quick read. They had been barred from the 1948 Olympics because of their part in World War II, and they had no sterling moments in gymnastics history to fall back on. Yet they got a lot of mileage out of one U.S. State Department trip in 1950 in which three American gymnasts flew over to Tokyo to acquaint the Japanese with the latest developments in international gymnastics. It was also a goodwill tour, arranged by General Douglas MacArthur, and it marked the first time a foreign team of any kind had set foot on Japanese soil since before Pearl Harbor. The crowds were tremendous—30,000 in Osaka one day—and the Japanese took the exhibition much more seriously than the Americans imagined. They filmed everything that moved, wrote down everything that was said, and, so it seemed later, perfected everything the Americans showed them—and much more. At the Helsinki Games, the Japanese placed four of their five gymnasts in the top twenty-five of the All-Around; the best U.S. finisher was thirtieth and the fourth best American was eighteenth.

The Japanese didn't beat the Russians in 1956 either, but that was mainly a consequence of the judging. Chukarin again won the All-Around, becoming the second gymnast in history—forty-four years after Italy's Braglia—to repeat. Takashi Ono of Japan was only .05 of a point back and nine of the first ten All-Arounders were either Russians or Japanese. In Rome in 1960, Ono was again beaten by .05, this time by Boris Shakhlin of the USSR, but nothing could help the Russians stave off the Japanese in the team championships. And nothing has worked ever since.

The Americans managed to grab fifth place in 1960, their highest finish ever. But in comparison to the Soviet Union and Japan, the United States has no gymnastics history. Only a past. For example, when Kurt Thomas did his thing at the 1978 World Championships in Strasbourg, much was made of the fact that this was the first U.S. gold medal in international competition in forty-six years, dating back to the 1932 Olympics. Except that the gymnastics competition at the 1932 Olympics in Los Angeles was another fiasco along the lines of 1900 and 1904. Nothing that happened there is of any historical significance.

The 1936 U. S. Olympic team. From left: Coach Joseph Oszy, Arthur Pitt, Chester Phillips, Alfred Jochim, Frank Haubold, Frederick Meyer, George Wheeler, Kenneth Griffin, Frank Cumiskey, Manager Herbert Forsell

Only seven countries competed in gymnastics and the total number of contestants (forty-six) was less than had competed in Athens in 1896. The United States did win five gold medals, but all five of them were won by single-event specialists who were petitioned into the Games to help flesh out the embarrassingly small field. One of the regular U.S. team members, "Little Alfred" Jochim, finished tenth in the All-Around. Jochim was another product of the Union City, New Jersey, turnverein and from 1925 to 1933 he was the finest gymnast in America. He also gained a measure of international fame when, as the official flagbearer for the 1936 Olympic delegation in Berlin, he refused to dip the Stars and Stripes to Hitler as the United States marched past the reviewing stand during the opening ceremonies. Jochim won a record seven NAAU titles during his career, but against the best gymnasts of the world in Berlin, he finished no better than eighty-third in the All-Around. This frustration continued for the next forty years until Peter Kormann, a student at Southern Connecticut State College, won a bronze medal in floor exercise at the 1976 Olympics in Montreal. However, at no time during those forty years did the United States place a gymnast in the top ten of the All-Around or do better than its fifth-place showing as a team in Rome. All of which explains why Thomas's gold medal in Strasbourg and his sixth-place finish there in the All-Around created such a stir around the world: It was a signal that the United States had made a quantum leap in international gymnastics.

What was it that the United States needed so badly —other than a Thomas—in order to be competitive? At one point during the AAU's administration of the sport, the grocery list would have included all of the following: more money, better organization, good coaching, knowledge of the rules, international tours, and—at the heart of the problem—a new governing body.

To get an idea of why the AAU must accept the blame for the United States's poor showing, let's visit their old offices in the Woolworth Building on lower Broadway in New York City and have a look. Say the year is 1945, and that Jim Simms and Dan Ferris, the administrative mainstays of the AAU, are out to lunch. On their salary, that probably means a hot dog at Nedick's. The offices—actually *rooms* would be a better description—are located on the twenty-third floor and there are three of them, one big and two little. The cubbyholes are for Simms and Ferris, the larger one is the war room where the fortunes of fifteen national and international sports are decided. Everything *smells* old and apparently file cabinets haven't been invented yet because all we can see are shelves and shelves crammed from floor to ceiling with handbooks, stat sheets, photographs, commission reports, travel itineraries, and all manner of printed page. The place is so exquisitely cluttered, in fact, that the Marx Brothers could have moved right in and shot the stateroom scene from A *Night at the Opera* without the prop men having to alter a single detail.

The AAU has always been referred to as an "umbrella organization" because it keeps so many sports under its jurisdiction at one time. Except that it has never had enough money to go around. As a result, sports such as track and field, swimming, and boxing receive most of the attention. For a long time the AAU's annual dues were only twenty-five cents, and that didn't produce enough revenue to pay many people outside the central office. Mainly the AAU stayed in business because of volunteers who did their own work during the week and the AAU's at night or on weekends. This system worked fine for an established American sport like track. But gymnastics had never achieved anything more than cult status in the United States, and that's why a lot of its supporters began to feel there wasn't room for gymnastics under the AAU umbrella.

To begin with, the top brass at the AAU never gave a damn about gymnastics. It didn't produce any revenue and they would have been just as happy with-

Frank Bare, the executive director of the United States Gymnastics Federation and the man most responsible for America's emergence as a gymnastics power

Peter Kormann's bronze medal in floor exercise at the 1976 Olympics was the first awarded to an American in forty-six years.

out it. Except that if one sport were allowed to break away and form its own separate national federation, others might follow. No, the AAU had been authorized by the FIG to be the sole American governing body for gymnastics, and it wasn't going to relinquish that power just for righteousness sake. So while its rivals traveled all over the world making a name for themselves in gymnastics, the United States stayed home and made do with the National AAUs. Though the first World Championships were held in 1903 and once every four years thereafter, the United States did not make its first appearance until 1958. If a foreign team asked to tour the States, the AAU told them they would have to pay their own way. If a foreign team was interested enough to come anyway, as a reward the AAU provided them with equipment that dated back to Ling and Jahn.

In 1962, a group of U.S. gymnastics people gave up trying to revamp the AAU's thinking and formed the USGF. Frank Bare was chosen to serve as executive director. Bare looked more like a tennis pro than an executive director of anything. But he had been a national champion in gymnastics while at the University of Illinois and he was familiar with money problems, having raised funds for the Tucson YMCA. At the time he was approached about the USGF position, he was turning a handsome profit in the insurance business, and as it turned out he knew how to sell gymnastics even better.

Bare's first office was located in a spare room just off his kitchen in Tucson and was smaller than either Simms's or Ferris's. But in six months it had become a war room in the battle against the AAU. In June 1963, the USGF held its own national championships at Maine East High School in Chicago. This was pure heresy as far as the AAU was concerned. It warned that any athletes who participated in this unauthorized competition would have their AAU travel cards revoked and, in all likelihood, would be ineligible for the 1964 Olympics in Tokyo. Because of the severity of the threat, the USGF could only get 100 top-flight men and women to participate. Rusty Mitchell was one of them, and he became a test case.

Mitchell went to Southern Illinois University and was probably the finest gymnast in America. He performed a daring double back flip on a quarter-inch mat during his floor exercise routine at the 1963 USGF meet and he wasn't afraid of the AAU either. He was willing to risk his future in gymnastics for two reasons: because his coach at SIU, Bill Meade, told him he owed it to himself and to the future of the sport; and because, down deep, both he and Meade thought the AAU was bluffing. The AAU said it wasn't, and after Mitchell competed in the 1963 USGF meet, it suspended him indefinitely.

Acting as though nothing had ever happened, Mitchell walked right up to the reception desk at the 1964 Olympic Trials and started to write down his name on a registration form.

"I'm sorry, Rusty," said the AAU man behind the desk, "but I was told not to allow you to register."

Mitchell turned to Meade and said, "What's going on?"

"I don't know," said Meade, "but don't worry. I'll go talk to Frank Cumiskey and see if he can straighten it out."

Of the volunteers who helped the AAU run gymnastics in those days, Cumiskey was one of the most knowledgeable and the most understanding. When Meade brought Mitchell's protest to ·him, he was anxious to suggest a compromise.

"It's simple, Bill," said Cumiskey. "Rusty participated in the 1963 USGF meet. That was an open competition and it wasn't sanctioned by the AAU. When one body is given the authority to run a sport, an athlete cannot go off and compete in open competition unless that ruling body, in this case the AAU, gives him permission. Rusty didn't have our permission. But if he wants to try out for the Olympic team, all he has to do is promise not to compete in any more USGF meets."

In the 1950s, American gymnasts were popular, if not always artistic.

Rusty Mitchell became a test case in the fight between the USGF and the Amateur Athletic Union.

Frank Cumiskey

Meade gave Mitchell the good news.

"You're kidding, that's all?"

"Yep."

So Mitchell walked up to Cumiskey, looked him right in the eye, and said, "I, Rusty Mitchell, promise never to compete in a USGF meet again."

"Are you sure?" said Cumiskey.

"Yessir, I'm sure," said Mitchell, who made the Olympic team, finished thirty-second at the Tokyo Games, and then went right back to competing in USGF meets.

Years later, the conversation still produces an ironic chuckle from Cumiskey, whose allegiance was hopelessly split between serving the best interests of gymnastics and serving those who had been empowered to run the sport.

"I knew Rusty never meant a word of his promise," says Cumiskey. "But in those days, the gymnastics people at the AAU were fighting just to keep the sport afloat. Even though we raised a stink with Rusty Mitchell, that's the reason we didn't keep him out of the Olympics."

By 1966, the AAU-USGF feud was being waged overseas. At the World Championships in Dortmund, West Germany, two different American teams showed up. One was the official AAU team, which competed and finished in sixth place. The other was a USGF delegation, which sat in the stands in protest and spent the rest of the time lobbying for FIG support. In 1968, the USGF took it upon itself to translate, print, and distribute the first English language version of the Code of Points, and since then more copies of it have been sold in the United States than in all the other countries of the world combined. This rather obscure fact may have helped turn the tide.

By October 1970, Bare had succeeded in getting the matter of who should control U.S. gymnastics on the agenda of an FIG executive committee meeting in Ljubljana, Yugoslavia. A vote would be taken among those committee members present and whoever received a majority, either the AAU or the USGF, would be the acknowledged ruling body. Before the vote was cast, Arthur Gander, the president of the FIG, asked Bare to speak in behalf of the USGF proposal. Bare said his piece, then turned and asked the attending secretary a question.

"How many Code of Points has the USGF sold in the last year?"

"Approximately six thousand."

"How many has the AAU sold?"

"Forty-two, I believe."

That did it. The vote was 20 to 8 in favor of the USGF.

The AAU-USGF feud lasted from 1962 to 1970, and while the ultimate decision did a great deal for the future of American gymnastics, the years of bickering, the bogus promises of allegiance, the two American teams at the same competition, the general confusion —all seemed to compound the problems and sap the dedication of the aspiring American gymnast. If this was a sport where you couldn't count on travel, victory, support, or fame, let alone gainful employment, why stick with it after college? Indeed, why treat it with respect while you were competing? Gymnastics wasn't on any firmer ground than sky diving. It was a lark from start to finish, and a lot of talented guys looked at it exactly that way. Get in and have some fun, get out and find something to do with your life. Except that some gymnasts had so much fun goofing off, they couldn't stop.

The specialists were the wildest, guys who concentrated on one or two events instead of the All-Around, guys who could afford to be daredevils. When they weren't in the gym doing double back flips on the hardwood floor, they were out cracking up their motorcycles, flying through automobile windshields, dying in crop dusters and, for those who survived, doing many of the same stunts over again for Hollywood, Vegas, or circus crowds.

Rusty Rock, the 1966 NCAA high bar champ from Cal State-Northridge, was an aerialist for "Circus Circus" in Las Vegas. Bob Dixon of Iowa, who missed the 1968 Olympic team because he totaled his car and himself on the way to the Trials, does a comedy routine on trampoline and diving board for circuses all over Europe. Buck Taylor made a living getting thrown through plate glass windows as one of Matt Dillon's deputies on *Gunsmoke*. Mark Davis of Southern Illinois was a high bar specialist in college, but he began to make a name for himself when he performed a quadruple back somersault on rings at the annual Santa Monica Gymfest on the beach outside Los Angeles. Davis has now turned to movies and has a quick scene with Mae West in *Sextette*, wherein the aging sex queen wanders into a gymnastics workout, takes one look at Davis up on the rings, and makes a typical Mae West remark about his anatomy. There were countless other crazies doing gymnastics during the Sixties, including Hal Shaw of Illinois, who did a Tsukahara vault in Big Ten competition while wearing a Red Baron helmet, goggles, and scarf. He was put up to it by his coach, Charlie Pond, who now runs a hot dog skiing school in Salt Lake City.

The most successful of the gymnast-cum-stuntmen is Brent Williams, who was a good but not great gymnast at Southern Illinois during the mid-1960s. Williams now lives in Los Angeles and could get along fine just by being a model and an actor in commercials. But he has also appeared in *Pete's Dragon*, where he did some dancing; on *Police Woman*, where he taught flips to Angie Dickinson; on *Fernwood Tonight*, where he wrestled; and on *Laverne & Shirley*, where he played a tumbler from a Hungarian circus. On any given day, Williams may get a call to go over and teach Angie Dickinson's daughter a new balance beam dismount, to bring his mini tramp over to the Playboy mansion to entertain some of Hef's guests, or to do a flip over George Gobel's convertible in a gasoline commercial.

"This isn't what I planned to do with my life," says Williams. "I figured I'd give gymnastics a whirl in college, then look for a sensible way to make a living. But something happened to me—or rather didn't happen to me—in college. I never lost the urge to *perform* in front of people. And I think part of the reason is that I never won enough, or at least not big enough for my own ego. I know it's different for Kurt Thomas, because I grew up in Miami, Florida, and I judged some of Kurt's meets when he was in high school. Hey, he's got *talent* like we never saw during my era. Sure, Rusty Mitchell could do a double back on the hardwood floor, but Thomas has a chance to become the best gymnast in the world. That would make anybody serious about what he was doing. Gymnastics in the Sixties was mainly fun. Nobody pushed really hard to be an international star because it was obvious that it wasn't there. The gymnasts I remember most from my era were mainly daredevils, like Frank Schmitz, a teammate of mine at SIU who was killed flying a crop duster. Then there is a trampoline freak named Dar Robinson who once did 125 back somersaults in a row. He's also jumped off the top of the Astrodome and landed in an air bag, and parachuted out of an airplane *in a car*. When I think of the Sixties, these are the kind of gymnasts I remember."

Jim Culhane was undoubtedly the most notorious. Not only because he streaked an NCAA meet, but because he hung on in gymnastics long after most coaches wanted him to quit—and continued to get better. If he hadn't, nobody would have put up with his hell-raising. But he was always just good enough to have a shot at making an international team.

In 1968, for example, he was looking pretty good at the Olympic Trials until one evening when he and his wife decided they couldn't stand to sit around the Ramada Inn in Colorado Springs. So Culhane hot-wired one of the team rental cars and they took off for a couple hours. When the coaches found out about it,

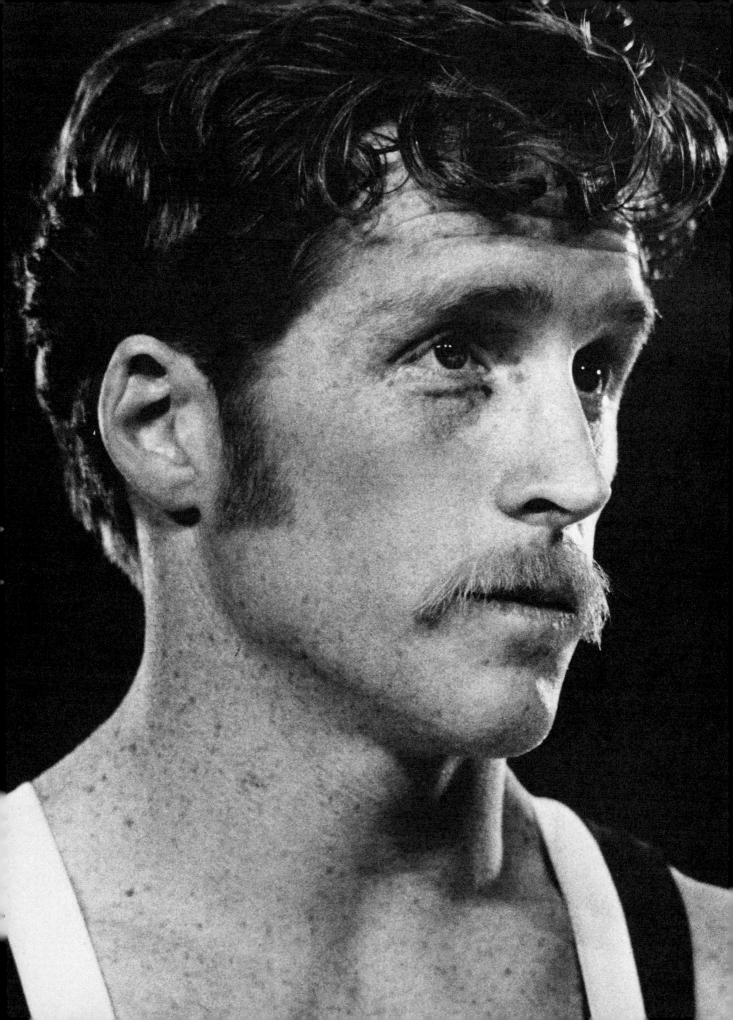

Jim Culhane, one of the most colorful and notorious personalities in gymnastics history

Mae West admires Mark Davis' form on rings in the movie, *Sextette*.

Brent Williams does a flip over George Gobel's convertible in a commercial for a gasoline company.

they weren't amused.

"What do you want, a plane ticket home or money?" they asked.

"The money," said Culhane, who then hitchhiked all over the country visiting old friends, eventually ending up in Mexico City where he sat in the stands and watched the 1968 Olympics.

Culhane went souvenir hunting one day during the 1971 Pan American Games in Cali, Colombia. He took a shine to an official Pan Am Games flag that was flying near the central pavilion. It was white with a red Aztec-Inca emblem, and he just had to have it. So he cut the rope, hauled down the flag, stuffed it into his U.S. warmups, and strolled off without any idea that he had started an international incident. A large band of Cubans had watched Culhane's little act of piracy and they weren't amused either. Culhane heard a lot of yelling in Spanish and turned around just in time to catch a haymaker in his horn-rimmed glasses. His head was cut just above the right eye and he might have been in real trouble if a group of Americans hadn't interceded in his behalf. The brouhaha was reported in newspapers all over the world and Culhane even made the network news back in the States. To escape twenty years at hard labor, he had to write a letter of apology to the Governor of the Pan Am village. In return, he was given a small souvenir flag he could have bought for half a peso at a concession stand.

Undeterred by the controversy, Culhane competed in the 1972 Olympics and was still in top shape as late as 1976, ten years after his graduation from Penn State. These days, Culhane is still pretty much a hitchhiker. He has taught gymnastics from Campbell, California, to the U.S. Military Academy at West Point, but he would like to land a permanent head coaching job so he can stay in the sport. Of course, if he can't find one here, he may follow the lead of Mark Davis, who, when he isn't cavorting with Mae West, is the national gymnastics coach of the Virgin Islands.

"I guess people still think I'm an oddball," says Culhane, "but the things I've done aren't unprecedented and some of the stories about me have begun to take on a life of their own. Take the streaking incident at the 1974 NCAAs. It was a popular fad back then and I picked up thirty-five dollars in dares just by doing it. Hell, the ancient Greeks used to do it for free. Then there was the story that said I had parachuted into a training camp in Heidelberg, West Germany. I've never even been to Heidelberg. Of course, I *have* parachuted in the nude."

Now there's something even the ancient Greeks never did.

Epilogue

It took Kurt Thomas eight years to prepare for his moment of opportunity in Strasbourg, the hardest part of which was in "being the first one out," as Bart Conner puts it. America had never produced a truly top-notch male gymnast for Thomas to pattern himself after, so when he needed someone to look to for inspiration after a particularly grueling week of training, Thomas had to presuppose his own stardom.

Perhaps this explains why, when he was given just sixty seconds to justify all those years of hard work and sacrifice, Thomas was able to respond with such a stunning floor exercise routine at the World Championships. Others might have been paralyzed by the pressure. But Thomas was convinced he would win before he even walked out on the mat. When they saw his performance the judges agreed, awarding him a 9.9, and the United States its first gold medal in the seventy-five-year history of the World Championships.

For all the attention lavished upon him since that moment, Thomas might as well have invented a new sport. And, in essence, he has. Until Strasbourg, the word *gymnastics* actually signified "women's gymnastics" in the minds of most Americans and of people all over the world. Long before Olga Korbut did her famous back flip off the uneven bars at the 1972 Olympics, the women had a much bigger following. At USGF meets in the 1960s, when the women rotated to another event on the other side of the arena, the entire crowd would get up and rotate to that side of the arena, too, leaving the men to perform for themselves. And after Nadia Comaneci's unprecedented string of 10.0s at the 1976 Montreal Games, the gap between the two wings of the sport widened even further. In the crush to get at Nadia, the press so ignored the men's All-Around champion, Nikolai Andrianov, that he found it almost amusing. "You learn to expect it," said Andrianov.

But now that Thomas has won something big in international circles, men's gymnastics has become a hot spectator sport in the United States, and an in-creasingly popular participatory sport as well. This doesn't mean that Roger Counsil's "Gladiator Syndrome" is a thing of the past, merely that it is now acceptable for an eight-year-old boy to forsake Little League baseball and Pee Wee Football in hopes of becoming "the next Kurt Thomas."

Thomas's return from France was not as triumphant as Charles Lindbergh's, but for someone who had spent most of his adolescence toiling in utter anonymity, it must have seemed so. Neither the media nor the entertainment business could get enough of Thomas. And the question of how to gain recognition for himself and his sport was no longer a problem. Men's gymnastics was suddenly extremely fashionable. The only problem for Kurt was knowing how to maneuver back and forth between the whirl of celebrity life and the real world of training, competing, and trying to make do as an amateur athlete.

In 1964, when he was the best gymnast America had to offer, Rusty Mitchell wrote a letter to Johnny Carson asking if he would be interested in having him on the *Tonight* show.

"I offered to perform a double back somersault right there on the stage if he didn't want to bother dragging out a lot of equipment," says Mitchell, who is now gymnastics coach at the University of New Mexico. "But I received a letter from an assistant producer telling me to forget it. I got the impression from his choice of words that he didn't know what men's gymnastics was."

In 1964 nobody did. But sure enough, on the night of November, 22, 1978, there was Kurt Thomas becoming a legitimate star in the only true manner in which Americans recognize you as one—when they can peek between their toes and see you on the TV screen next to Johnny Carson.

Like Dick Cavett, who used to write jokes for him, Carson had fooled around with gymnastics as a kid and he knew enough about the movements to play them for laughs with Thomas. He mugged for the camera whenever Kurt did something that looked painful, fell twice on purpose as Kurt was trying to hold him up in a handstand, and turned the act into something worthy of "The Mighty Carson Art Players." Thomas got several rounds of applause for the gold medal he had won in France three weeks earlier, then excused himself as any true star would in order to have dinner with some independent producer who wanted to make a movie of his life.

From these heights, Kurt and Beth returned to their little house trailer on Rural Route 27 in Terre Haute to find their water pipes frozen solid. They couldn't even go to the bathroom, much less wash the dirty dishes they had left in the sink when they dashed off to California. As far as Kurt knew, this was a predicament which none of Carson's other guests faced upon returning home. But for an amateur athlete in the United States, it was just about par. The United States is the only country in the world that does not subsidize the efforts of its amateur athletes once they leave college. And for an undergraduate like Thomas, who married and moved out of the dorm, things were no better. There wasn't much the athletic department at Indiana State could do for Kurt beyond his $130-a-month scholarship—which provided him and Beth with exactly $16.25 apiece per week to spend for food, gas, and a roof over their heads. Any way you slice it, it ain't much.

To help make ends meet, Kurt sold the last vestiges of his bachelor days—his waterbed and his used 240Z; Beth started working mornings as a secretary in the athletic department and afternoons teaching gymnastics at the local Girls Club. What with both of them going to school full time and Kurt locked into his demanding schedule of training and competing, the couple occasionally found time for a goodnight kiss. Otherwise, every minute of the day was spoken for.

When the water pipes froze, it threw everything out of whack. Kurt scraped together fifty dollars to hire a plumber, who dug through the layers of ice and snow that engulfed the trailer and wrapped heat-conducting tapes around the pipes. That did the trick, and for a week and a half the Thomases had running water and full potty privileges. Then while they were on campus one day, Sarge, the family Doberman pinscher, dug through the layers of ice and snow that engulfed the trailer and ate the heat tapes. Spending another fifty bucks was out of the question, and Kurt wasn't about to risk sticking his valuable hands into some slush hole. So, being young and a bit feisty, Kurt and Beth decided they would just forget about the frozen pipes for a while and concentrate on more important things. Here, then, is the scene at the Thomas household as Kurt moved into his final week of training in preparation for the 1978 World Cup competition in Sao Paulo, Brazil:

Beth's alarm goes off at 6:00 A.M., but Kurt stays under the covers until the last possible moment. At this hour of the morning the temperature in the Thomas's mini bedroom seems to rival the 8-degree reading outside. Part of the problem is that the trailer has no skirt on the bottom to act as insulation against the cold. The location of the trailer park doesn't help either. R.R. 27 runs through a flat and desolate area next to Interstate 70, so each night brings high winds and deeper snowdrifts—not to mention a nonstop convoy of trucks barreling toward St. Louis or Indianapolis.

By 7:15, Kurt and Beth are on the way to school in their blue Chevy van, the one which was recently totaled in a traffic accident but restored to good running order by a sympathetic insurance agent. In this weather, it can take twenty minutes to get to campus and if, on arrival, Kurt and Beth seem to hurry inside Hulman Arena, it's not just because it's cold outside. Keep in mind the no-water situation at the trailer; neither of them has been to the bathroom since they left Hulman at 10 o'clock last night. Blessed relief is ahead.

Beth has learned to think of the women's locker

Kurt does his V-seat for Johnny
Carson.

Washing dishes at the trailer with
bottled water

room as her own bathroom. She takes all her showers there, washes her hair there, changes clothes there, and puts her makeup on there before hurrying down the hall to her 8 A.M. job as a typist in the intramural office. Kurt will spend most of the morning working out in the little gym. He returns from class in time to practice with the Indiana State team from 3 to 6 P.M. After a break for dinner at the Bonanza Steak House, he comes back and does stretching exercises until 10. *Every day* he and Beth go through this same routine, and nobody on the team can figure out how they keep going with no water at home.

"For one thing, we're never there," says Beth. "Kurt lives on planes and in gyms. Besides, nothing bothers him outside gymnastics."

The amazing thing is that Beth really doesn't mind either. In a situation where most normal spouses—male or female—would be begging mommy and daddy for financial aid, she swallows most of her gripes and makes the best of things. Not because she likes it, but because she's a tough farm girl willing to tolerate most any inconvenience for a while, if doing so will help Kurt set up a long-term career in gymnastics. Right now, that's the most important thing in both their lives.

"So we dirty a few dishes at home and have to buy a couple gallons of bottled water to clean them up, so what?" she says. "It's kind of like living in pioneer days."

Apparently nothing does bother Kurt outside gymnastics, because he went off to Sao Paulo and placed second in the World Cup All-Around, beating in the process two of the five men who finished above him in Strasbourg. He passed Eizo Kenmotsu of Japan, a nine-time Olympic medalist who was second in France, and Eberhard Gienger of West Germany, who was fourth.

Despite the obvious confidence he has in himself and the mercurial manner in which he dispenses tricks during a meet, Thomas has never overestimated his worth as a gymnast. When he won the 1978 USGF title in Los Angeles and was thinking ahead to the World Championships, he rated himself no better than ninth in the world—and he apologized in case that sounded cocky. When he ended up sixth in Strasbourg, despite a couple of foul-ups during compulsories, he said he thought he could move up to third within a year. Yet here he was in Brazil, nine weeks later, sitting in the No. 2 spot and feeling for the very first time as though he were on the verge of becoming No. 1.

For the sake of argument, let's say that Thomas was No. 2A. He and the man who beat him in Brazil, Russia's Alexander Ditiatin, were separated by only a tenth of a point, but the real No. 1 man ducked the meet entirely. That would be Nikolai Andrianov of the Soviet Union. His absence peeved Kurt, but it made perfect sense from Andrianov's point of view: Why should the heavyweight champion of gymnastics risk his title in *South America*?

If you think you can take Andrianov, you'd better do it at the World Championships or the Olympics, because otherwise he's very careful about picking his meets and his opponents. Thomas was reminded of the time early in 1978 when he heard via the grapevine that Andrianov feared him more than any other gymnast in the world. "Yeah, well then he must be more worried about me now than ever."

It was when he returned from the World Cup that Thomas's career became a press agent's dream and a travel agent's nightmare. For the first four months of 1979 he was on the go nearly every day—hopping planes, winning meets, posing for pictures, talking gymnastics, and meeting some of the most famous people in the world.

On January 6, Thomas kicked off his whirlwind tour by flying to New Mexico for the Albuquerque Journal Invitational, a meet directed by Rusty Mitchell. Before a two-night crowd of 30,000—the largest ever to watch men's gymnastics in this country—Kurt won four of six events and the All-Around title. He could just about see Albuquerque again three days later as he passed by at 37,000 feet en route to an appearance on the Dinah Shore show in Los Angeles. He did a few on-camera flips with Brianne Leary of *Chips*, then he and Beth had dinner with another Hollywood type who had visions of doing a movie about him.

When the Thomases returned home the next day, there was still snow on the ground and ice in their pipes, but something new had been added—the crew from ABC that was camped out on their doorstep waiting to shoot a "quick" interview segment for *Wide World of Sports*. Needless to say, "quick" turned out to be seven hours of filming and talking, but mostly laughing, as nine people and all kinds of cameras and lighting equipment tried to squeeze into the Thomas's nine by twelve foot living room. There at the end— when Sarge had been brought in from the cold to have his picture taken, and the people in the crew had run in and out twenty-five times for food and pit stops—the place was in hysterics.

The next day, January 12, promised to be an intriguing one because Andrianov was actually going to venture into Kurt's backyard. The Russian men's and women's teams had come to the United States for an exhibition tour and would be performing for one night only in Indianapolis, an hour and a half drive from Terre Haute. Thomas had been asked by the promoters to make a special appearance with them. That meant No. 1, No. 2, and No. 2A would all be on the Market Square Arena floor at the same time. While no scores would be handed out, a lot of points could be won or lost in the psychological warfare department.

If Andrianov believed something important was at stake, you couldn't guess it from the master-of-all-he-surveys look that he gave to the enthusiastic Indiana crowd. He looked both regal and intimidating in heavy black gloves, bright red trunks, and a matching T-shirt stretched tight over his bulging chest that said "Tumble and Trample" on the front. War games or not, Kurt felt he had to act like an unofficial host to Andrianov because of their relative stature in the sport and because this was practically his home turf. So at what he thought was an appropriate moment during warmups, he made a point of saying a good-natured and well-intentioned hello. Andrianov looked at him with absolutely no trace of recognition. When Thomas repeated his greeting, he pretended not to understand.

"Maybe it's part of their training in the Soviet Union," says Thomas, "but Andrianov has never shown me any respect. He and I competed in the same All-Around group at the 1976 Olympics. He would nudge me, bump into me, even jump in front of me in line during warmups. Then he made some comment to me in Russian and all his teammates laughed. When he won the gold medal, I tried to congratulate him again, but he just shunned me. I don't know why, because I was certainly no threat to him back then. But I'm sure he was playing some kind of tactical game designed to intimidate me; Sergei Khizniakov tried the very same tricks on me when we were up at West Point training for the 1978 American Cup. Andrianov was no different in Strasbourg, but at least there it made some sense: When you've won gold medals in floor exercise at two straight Olympics, you don't want to lose to an American in the World Championships. His attitude bugs me, but it also gets me going. What I like hearing most is that he fears me."

Both gymnasts went their separate ways without an international incident, and the next day Kurt got more than his share of recognition. First he won the All-Around competition in a dual meet against Arizona State that was being taped by Home Box Office. Then he went across the street to Pizza City and got a standing ovation from a hundred ISU students who had gathered there to watch a replay of his gold-medal winning performance in Strasbourg. When ABC's Jim McKay said, "Kurt Thomas of Miami, Florida, and Indiana State University has won the . . ." that's all you could hear for the screaming and the cheering and

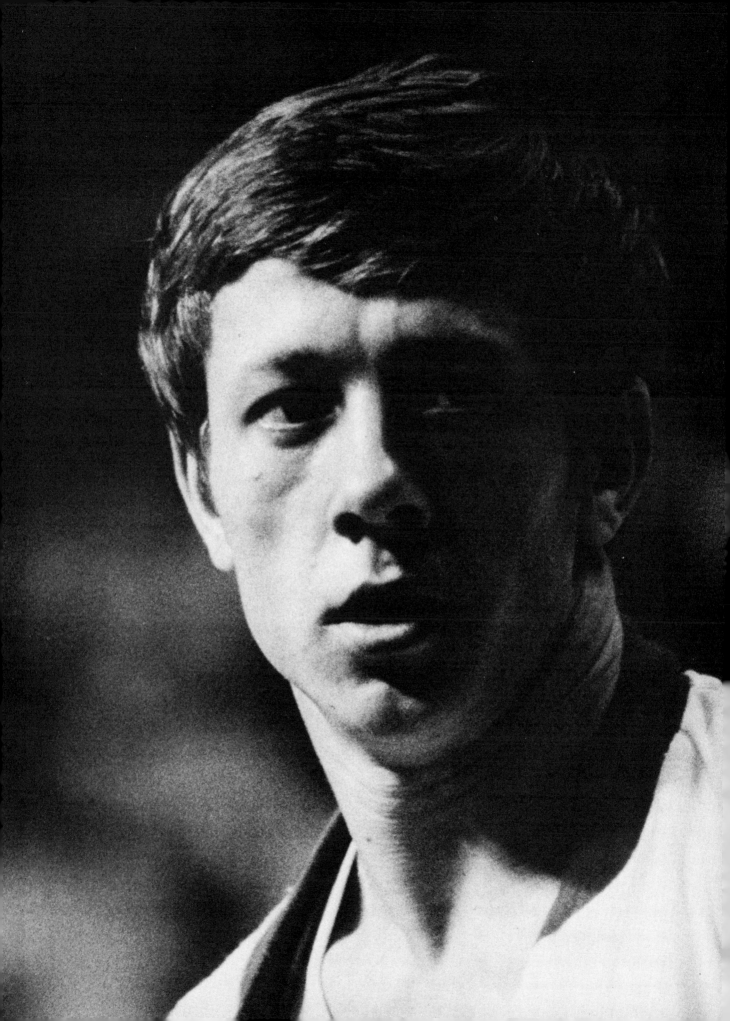

The New York Times Magazine
APRIL 29, 1979/SECTION 6

NEW FLAIR IN GYMNASTICS

Kurt Thomas
Performing on the
Pommel Horse

THE DEPARTMENT
STORE AS THEATER

A seemingly impossible achievement for an American male gymnast: the cover of *The New York Times Magazine*
At the White House
National Youth Awards

the pitchers of beer crashing against the wall.

When the traveling suddenly let up and editors discovered that Thomas was going to be stationary for a few days, the print media blitz began. It was led by *Life* photographer John Zimmerman, who set records for most time on the job (thirteen days—sometimes round the clock—on two separate trips from L.A.), most equipment ("half a ton," he said), and most chances taken (Thomas had to beg him not to climb out on a ledge forty feet above the floor because he didn't want a photographer's death on his conscience). *Time, Look, The New York Times Magazine,* the *Christian Science Monitor*—all these and many more would follow in the next few weeks. But when Zimmerman finally left on January 31, Kurt was dead on his feet and fresh out of Thomas Flairs for anybody's camera. That's when Mother Nature stepped in and zapped him with a head cold, and Roger Counsil mercifully scratched his name off the traveling squad for a meet at Penn State.

It wasn't long before the hectic schedule began again. Kurt and Beth went on a four-day spree, which—for sheer snob appeal—rivals anything Barbara Walters ever did. This time, however, we will sneak a peek at Beth's diary, and see the glamorous life from her point of view.

Thursday, Feb. 22
Terre Haute/The White House/
New Orleans/Baton Rouge

We had to wake up at five o'clock in the morning to get on a private jet that was taking us to meet Jimmy Carter.

Birch Bayh, the senator from Indiana, had arranged the whole thing. Except when we got to the Washington, D.C., area it was too foggy to land. We circled for an hour and a half, then finally gave up on National Airport and landed at Dulles, which is somewhere in Virginia. We got to ride in a chauffeur-driven limousine, but there were seven of us and we ran into bumper-to-

bumper traffic like I have never seen. It took us two and a half hours to get to Senator Bayh's office, and I'd say we spent no more than five minutes with the President.

He was very, very nice to us, but all I could think of when I saw him shaking hands with Kurt was, "God, can you imagine how many people like us he has to meet every day, five minutes at a time!"

We ate a quick lunch with Senator Bayh, then jumped in a cab and got trapped in another traffic jam on the way to the airport. We made our four P.M. flight to Baton Rouge, where Kurt is going to compete in the Mardi Gras gymnastics competition tomorrow night. But when we got there, they had fog, too. We had to land in New Orleans, then rent a car and drive two hours in the rain to Baton Rouge. We went straight to the arena so Kurt could work out. He didn't get finished until after eleven P.M. We were both starving, so we ran two blocks in the rain to a Shoney's. My dress faded.

Friday, Feb. 23
Baton Rouge

Woke up at six A.M. so Kurt could have some breakfast and get squared away about tonight's meet before going over to the arena and stretching out. I went window shopping for a while, but spent most of the day sleeping.

Kurt got a 9.9 at the meet tonight. It was on horse and it was the fifth of his career, I think. One judge, Gene Wettstone of Penn State, even gave him a 10.0! We celebrated by going to Shoney's again.

Saturday, Feb. 24
Baton Rouge/Los Angeles

We got up at five A.M. to catch a flight to L.A., where Kurt is going to appear on Bob Hope's National Youth Awards special. We made our flight, but there was something wrong with the plane and we had to stop in Dallas to get it fixed. We got to California two hours late, then had lunch with some guy who wanted Kurt to play a Russian gymnast in an episode of *Paper Chase*. He had to say no because he would have missed too much of Indiana State's schedule.

The Bob Hope show took forever to do. We were there from three in the afternoon until ten at night, just for Kurt's little segment. But we did get to meet Bob Hope and Lucille Ball, who presented an award to Kurt.

Sunday, Feb. 25
L.A./Indianapolis

We got out of bed at five A.M., made our flight to Indianapolis, but couldn't land there because the runway was covered with ice. It took them four hours to get the plane down on the ground—in Dayton. We sat there on the runway for three hours while they de-iced the brakes. Then, when we were next in line for takeoff, the plane ahead of us skidded off the runway. When we finally landed in Indianapolis, it was after ten P.M.

All the roads to Terre Haute were closed. Kurt called every hotel in the area and finally got the last room at the Sheraton. I couldn't believe it. What a trip.

A lot of new things were coming up for Kurt in 1979 —a kiss from Angie Dickinson on NBC's Olympic telethon, an appearance on *Good Morning America*, a whole show with Dick Cavett, and a weekend trip to the Bahamas for ABC's Superstars competition. There were also some rather nice old things in the offing, such as his repeat victory at the American Cup in New York and a big revenge win over Conner at the NCAAs in Baton Rouge, where Thomas got another 9.9 (on parallel bars) and another 10.0 from one of the judges.

Then, a few weeks after he finished up at Indiana State, Thomas was reunited with his high school coach, Don Gutzler. They got together at the National Sports Festival in Colorado Springs and made plans for Gutzler to become at least a part-time coach and adviser again. The deal made sense because Kurt had decided to go to graduate school at Arizona State in Tempe; Gutzler, who now owns two gymnastics camps in Tucson, would be only 100 miles away.

Naturally, Gutzler started right in with the advice. "What is a shrimp like you gonna do at the Superstars?" he said. "You can't beat the football players at weight lifting, your legs are too short to keep up with the basketball players in a race, and you'll probably fall during the cycling competition and break your arm. You're a gymnast, not a superstar, and you better remember that!"

Seeing Gutzler again and hearing the old banter made Thomas stop and think about where he had been the last five years.

"I guess you could say I've grown up a bit since I dumped salad in my lap at the Indiana State athletic banquet, or when I could scarcely say my name on the Phil Donahue show. I've now met the President of the United States, drunk champagne in Spain, played pinballs in France, and watched Counsil eat fried squid that he thought was onion rings. A couple in New Jersey even named one of their twin sons after me. It has been a real experience.

"Winning the gold medal in France obviously meant a great deal to me personally. But I never anticipated what an impact it would have on men's gymnastics as a whole. Just before I was about to be introduced as a guest on the *Tonight* show, I started thinking how concerned I had been about having 'The Star-Spangled Banner' played at international meets. But now I am considered enough of a mainstream sports personality to be appearing with Johnny Carson. He said my name, I walked out on the stage, and there we were talking about the Flair and everything in front of twenty million people. Johnny said to me, 'Kurt, have you ever had any injuries in gymnastics?' I told him, 'Nothing serious, although I did fracture my neck once.' Right away he starts giving the audience that look of his.

"I said to myself right then: 'That wasn't so bad. It's all been worth it.'"

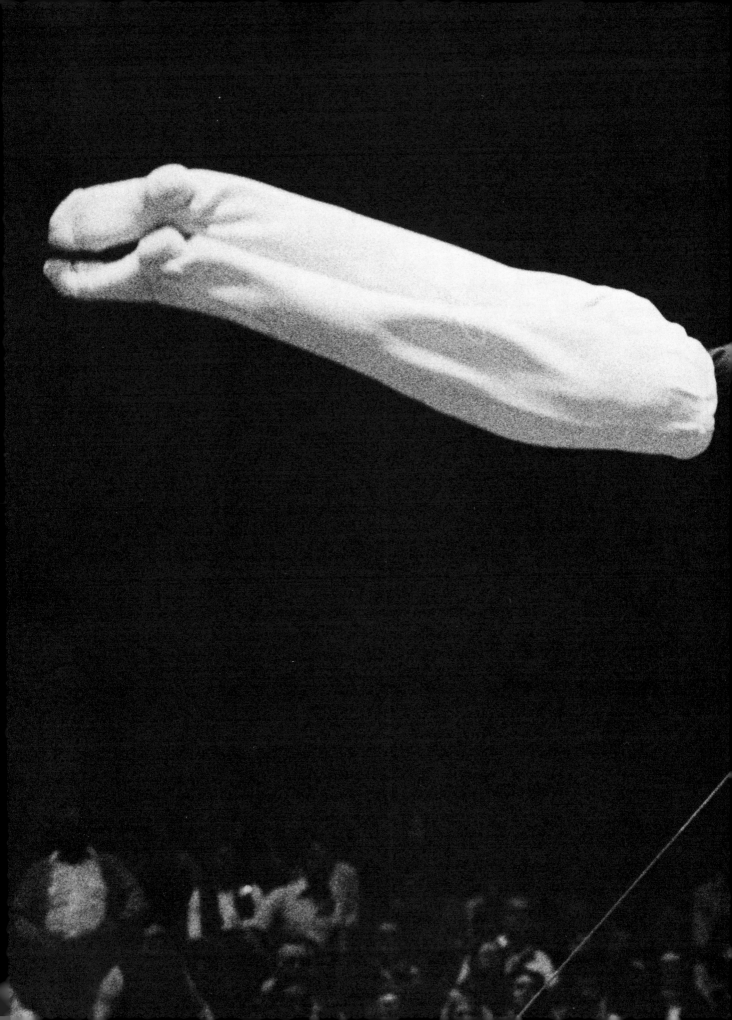

Gallery

Kurt Thomas is at home on any of the six events;
a world-class All-Arounder has to be. But while he is
merely "good" on rings and the vault, he is always a threat
to score 9.9 on the other four. The following
sequences show what make him so special on
floor, horse, parallel bars and high bar.

Floor Exercise

Borrowing the move he invented for the pommel horse, Kurt does the Thomas Flair in the midst of his floor exercise. To see how he gets into it, check the diagram above (section E specifically) which reenacts Thomas' gold-medal winning performance at the 1978 World Championships in Strasbourg.

Roundoff, flip flop 1½ twisting 1¾ somersault rolling out to a straddle jump sideways to land on left foot.

Undercircle right leg to support on the left leg, turning to a stand. Roundoff, Arabian dive roll, straddle press to a handstand, forward pirouette.

C Stoop-through to supine position, then with support from the fingertips press up to a V-seat. Straddle press to a handstand and controlled pike down to a stand. Roundoff, flip-flop, double-back somersault (tucked) to . . .

D⟶

. . . Half-turn to prone fall, then circling the legs to . . .

198

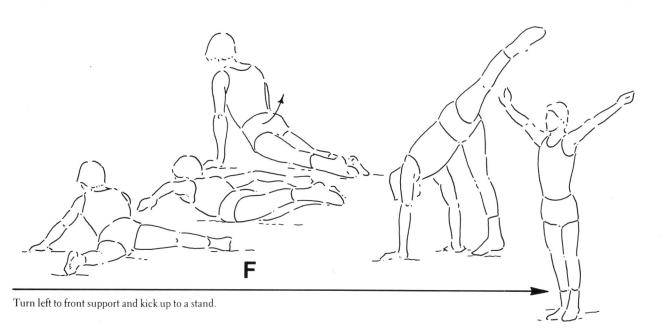

F

Turn left to front support and kick up to a stand.

E

. . . Splits. Double leg circles to begin the Thomas Flair on the floor, ending up in splits again.

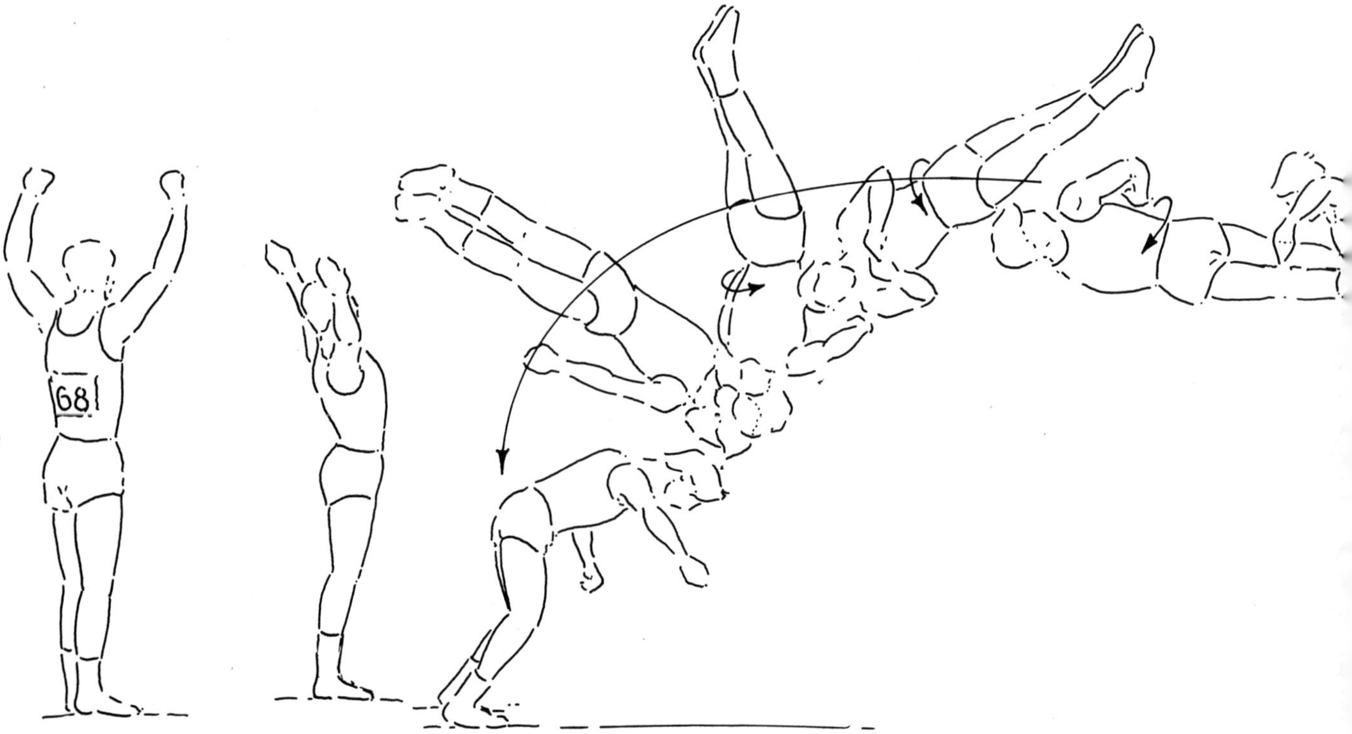
68

Roundoff, double-twisting back somersault.

G

Pommel Horse

Though the Thomas Flair has become a standard part of most world-class pommel horse routines, no one does it quite like its inventor. Kurt not only takes it around both sides of the apparatus, he also shows more extension and amplitude than anyone else in the world. The following sequence proceeds from top to bottom on each page.

Parallel Bars

A standard parallel bars routine must contain at least 11 different value parts of varying difficulty which must, in turn, be squeezed into roughly a 40-second performance. Here Thomas begins with a straddle press to a handstand on one bar.

Straddle press

Handstand

Diamido

Stutz

Conventional handstand

ck toss

Peach basket

Front uprise

Double-back dismount

fect landing

Congratulations from Coach Roger Counsil

High Bar

Thomas won a gold medal for his high bar routine at the 1979 World Championships in Fort Worth, scoring a 9.9. But at the 1980 American Cup in New York he went himself one better, scoring what for men is almost unheard of — a perfect 10.0. Here we pick up his routine as he does a back uprise to a handstand.

talder half-turn

Giant swings to build up momentum for a full-over. When gymnasts like Stoyan Deltchev of Bulgaria began soaring above the high bar to do flyaway half somersaults, Thomas had to throw out a move like the full-over and change his routine to show he could keep up — just as Deltchev and others had to do when he unveiled the Thomas Flair.

217

The full-over: getting ready for it, throwing it and catching it

A stoop-in

Coming out of the stoop-in, preparing for German giants   A kip change to . . .

. . . reverse grip giant swings   Half-in, half-out dismount

Looking for the mat

Sticking the dismount

Turning on the crowd

CREDITS:

All photographs by Rafael Beer except the following.

8-9 Alan E. Burrows   16 (left) Mary Ann Carter.   20 Bob
Kadel.   21 (top) Shelley Keever.   23 Alan E. Burrows.   27 Don
Chadez.   30 Don Morley.   34-35 Don Perdue.   36 *International
Gymnast.*   38 Don Perdue.   42 Steve Sisney.   47 Kent Hannon.
51 Bob Kadel.   55 Don Perdue.   56 Janice Higgins.   58 Steve Sisney.
59 Steve Sisney.   65 (top) Dick Criley.   67 (left) Courtesy of Penn State,
(right) Fred Turoff.   69 Don Chadez.   72 (top) *International Gymnast.*
74 Alan E. Burrows.   84 (top right) Rich Kenney.   88 Richard Endo.
90 (bottom right) Rich Kenney.   96 Courtesy of
Sterling Publishing.   99 (bottom) Alan E. Burrows.   100 Alan E.
Burrows.   103 Sheila Howorth.   105 Bob Kadel.   108 Glenn
Sundby.   110-11 Ray Lorenz.   113 *International Gymnast.*
114 (top left) Courtesy of Penn State, (top right) Rich Kenney.
115 Don Perdue.   120 Rich Kenney.   121 Courtesy of Penn State.
122 (top left) *International Gymnast.*   123 Bob Kadel.   126 (bottom)
Bob Kadel.   134 Glenn Sundby.   135 (right) Rich Kenney.   138 (top)
Alan E. Burrows.   139 (right) Kent Hannon, (left) *International
Gymnast.*   142 (second from left) Kent Hannon, (fourth from left) Kent
Hannon.   143 (top middle) Kent Hannon, (bottom) Rich Kenney.
147 (left) Kent Hannon.   154 Radio Times Hulton Picture Library.
156 Radio Times Hulton Picture Library.   157 Radio Times Hulton
Picture Library.   160 Kuntshistorische Museum, Vienna.   161 Radio
Times Hulton Picture Library.   162 (top) Courtesy of Penn State,
(bottom) Courtesy of Penn State.   165 Courtesy of Penn State.
166 Courtesy of Penn State.   167 Courtesy of Penn State.   168 (top)
Kent Hannon, (bottom) Tom Wakeling.   170 Courtesy of Penn
State.   171 (left) Courtesy of Rusty Mitchell, (right) Courtesy of Frank
Cumiskey.   173 (right) Rich Kenney, (left) Tom Sauters.
174 Courtesy of Penn State.   175 (left) Crown International Pictures,
(right) Courtesy of Brent Williams.   176 Scott Dine.
183 *International Gymnast.*   185 (bottom) Don Perdue.   186 ©1979
by The New York Times Company.   187 (left) Charlie Green, States
News Service.   189 (top) Courtesy of Louisiana State.   190-91 Bob
Kadel.   192 Ray Lorenz.   202-09 Glenn Sundby.   216-23 Bob
Kadel.

The following photographs are from the collection of Kurt Thomas: 62;
64 (left and right); 65 (bottom); 66; 70; 72 (bottom).

Line drawings 193-201 by A. B. Frederick of *International Gymnast.*